I dedicate this book to my daughter Jennifer Burleson, and my son, Andrew Burleson, since my royalty money will be helping to pay their College Tuition.

Donald K. Burleson

Oracle Silver Bullets
Real-World Oracle Performance Secrets

By Donald K. Burleson

Copyright © 2005 by Rampant TechPress. All rights reserved.

Printed in the United States of America.

Published in Kittrell, North Carolina, USA.

Oracle In-focus Series: Book 23

Series Editor: Donald Burleson

Editors: Janet Burleson, John Lavender, and Robin Haden

Production Editor: Teri Wade

Cover Design: Bryan Hoff

Printing History: April, 2005 for First Edition

ISBN: 0-9759135-2-2

Library of Congress Control Number: 2005901257

Oracle Silver Bullets
Real-World Oracle Performance Secrets

Oracle In-Focus Series

Donald K. Burleson

Table of Contents

Silver Bullets

Using the Online Code Depot

Purchase of this book provides complete access to the online code depot that contains the sample code scripts. All of the code depot scripts in this book are available for download in zip format, ready to load and use and are located at the following URL:

rampant.cc/bullet.htm

If technical assistance is needed with downloading or accessing the scripts, please contact Rampant TechPress at info@rampant.cc.

Are you WISE?

Get the premier Oracle tuning tool. The Workload Interface Statistical Engine for Oracle provides unparallel capability for time-series Oracle tuning, unavailable nowhere else.

Download now!

WISE supplements Oracle Enterprise Manager and it can quickly plot and spot performance signatures to allow you to see hidden trends, fast. WISE interfaces with STATSPACK or AWR to provide unprecedented proactive tuning insights. Best of all, it is only $9.95 for the Standard Edition and $199.95 for the Enterprise Edition. Get WISE.

www.wise-oracle.com

Get the Oracle Script Collection

This is the complete Oracle script collection from Mike Ault and Donald Burleson, the world's best Oracle DBA's.

Packed with over 500 ready-to-use Oracle scripts, this is the definitive collection for every Oracle professional DBA. It would take many years to develop these scripts from scratch, making this download the best value in the Oracle industry.

It's only $39.95 (less than 7 cents per script!). For immediate download go to:

www.oracle-script.com

Conventions Used in this Book

It is critical for any technical publication to follow rigorous standards and employ consistent punctuation conventions to make the text easy to read.

However, this is not an easy task. Within Oracle there are many types of notation that can confuse a reader. Some Oracle utilities such as STATSPACK and TKPROF are always spelled in CAPITAL letters, while Oracle parameters and procedures have varying naming conventions in the Oracle documentation. It is also important to remember that many Oracle commands are case sensitive, and are always left in their original executable form, and never altered with italics or capitalization.

Parameters - All Oracle parameters will be lowercase italics. Exceptions to this rule are parameter arguments that are commonly capitalized (KEEP pool, TKPROF), these will be left in ALL CAPS.

Variables – All PL/SQL program variables and arguments will also remain in lowercase italics (*dbms_job, dbms_utility*).

Tables & dictionary objects – All data dictionary objects are referenced in lowercase italics (*dba_indexes, v$sql*). This includes all *v$* and *x$* views (*x$kcbcbh, v$parameter*) and dictionary views (*dba_tables, user_indexes*).

SQL – All SQL is formatted for easy use in the code depot, and all SQL is displayed in lowercase. The main SQL terms (select, from, where, group by, order by, having) will always appear on a separate line.

Programs & Products – All products and programs that are known to the author are capitalized according to the vendor specifications (IBM, DBXray, etc). All names known by Rampant TechPress to be trademark names appear in this text as initial caps. References to UNIX are always made in uppercase.

Acknowledgements

This type of highly technical reference book requires the dedicated efforts of many people. Even though we are the authors, our work ends when we deliver the content. After each chapter is delivered, several Oracle DBAs carefully review and correct the technical content. After the technical review, experienced copy editors polish the grammar and syntax.

The finished work is then reviewed as page proofs are turned over to the production manager, who arranges the creation of the online code depot and manages the cover art, printing distribution, and warehousing.

In short, the authors play a small role in the development of this book, and we need to thank and acknowledge everyone who helped bring this book to fruition:

Robert Tuttle, for the production management, including the coordination of the cover art, page proofing, printing, and distribution.

Teri Wade, for her help in the production of the page proofs.

Bryan Hoff, for his exceptional cover design and graphics.

Janet Burleson, for her assistance with the web site, and for creating the code depot and the online shopping cart for this book.

Mike Ault, for his expert technical review of the content.

Supplemental Materials

Purchase of this book entitles the reader to free copies of important supplemental materials that will help with Oracle tuning and management:

- Free Oracle10g DBA Reference Poster   (an $8.95 value).

- Free copy of the Workload Interface Statistical Engine (WISE) for Oracle   (a $9.95 value).

 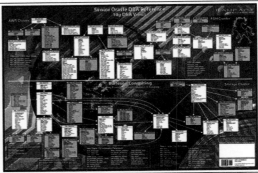

These reference tools are designed to aid in quickly accessing the complex Oracle10g workload structures.

The WISE software download will be available immediately and there is only a $5.99 charge for the shipping and handling of the poster.

To get the poster and WISE Oracle software, just go here:

www.rampant.cc/10g_customer

Coupon code is: wisese

Preface

Every Oracle professional should feel the exhilaration of making a single change and seeing the performance of their entire database improve. It's these types of silver bullets that can make you a hero in your shop and amaze your friends and associates.

All Oracle tuning professionals know that they must start by optimizing the database as a whole before tuning individual SQL statements. Only after you have tuned the external hardware (disk RAID, network, OS kernel parms) and the instance (indexes, CBO statistics, optimal parameter settings), is it appropriate to drill-down and tune individual SQL statements and application code.

We will see that a single change to an optimizer parameter can improve the behavior of hundreds of SQL statements, and database-wide tuning approaches such as adding a missing index, creating a materialized view or adjusting CBO statistics can make a significant difference in overall Oracle performance.

Many of these silver-bullet recommendations have been codified inside the Oracle 10g Automatic Database Diagnostic Monitor (ADDM), and the Automatic Memory Management (AMM) features, and every Oracle professional must recognize the benefits of these important tuning techniques.

In this book I share some of my in-the trenches Oracle tuning secrets. I include my actual techniques and tips, and demonstrate how to perform system-level tuning on all Oracle databases, from small OLTP systems to giant data warehouses.

In order to emphasize the main points of each silver bullet, I have deliberately simplified and over-generalized the problem.

As a teacher I know how important it is to clearly explain a problem, and students often get caught-up in minutiae if I present too much superfluous information.

In the interest of simplicity and clarity I have deliberately simplified the top 5 timed events reports, omitted "noise" from reports and use contrived, artificial examples to illustrate each technique.

Oracle tuning is both an "art" and a "pseudo-science". In the real-world of Oracle tuning, every situation is different and it is not uncommon for several independent factors to influence sub-optimal Oracle performance.

Oracle tuning is a semi-structured task and can never be fully-automated. Even Oracle Corporation has acknowledged that their Automatic Database Diagnostic Monitor and SQLTuning advisors cannot detect and suggest corrections for complex performance issues. Human intuition (hunches), years of real-world tuning experience all contribute to the illusion of "expert intuition" that always distinguishes an Oracle tuning guru.

Applying heuristics ("rules of thumb") to an Oracle tuning problem is a powerful technique, and even though a heuristic may not apply to every situation, understanding the general behavior of Oracle provides a baseline for your Oracle tuning knowledge, a launching-point for advanced Oracle tuning.

It is my sincere hope that this book will guide you through some basic system-wide tuning techniques and help you understand how the sundry Oracle components contribute to overall database performance.

Donald K. Burleson

Oracle Silver Bullets

CHAPTER 1

Silver bullets are often seen as magical

The Mysterious Oracle DBA

To management and the IT staff, the Oracle DBA is shrouded in mystery. They can be aloof, speak in indecipherable acronyms and manage their databases with cryptic scripts and tools. Of course, there is no magic to Oracle tuning, but there are techniques that can change the behavior of an entire database. Throughout this book, the term "silver bullet" will be used to describe any small DBA action that has a dramatic effect on the performance of a large portion of an Oracle database.

There are many silver bullets for Oracle performance tuning. A silver bullet simply contains a small set of commands that quickly relieves an acute performance bottleneck. Some of these just-in-time tuning techniques have been codified in Oracle10g via the Automatic Memory Management (AMM) facility, in which the SGA regions are changed dynamically to meet the changing demands of the application.

While there is no substitute for good database design, well-coded PL/SQL and optimized SQL, the Oracle DBA often has no control over the quality of these components. Silver bullets are sometimes the only solutions that remain for the Oracle DBA for any number of reasons.

Tight-Fisted Management

Management will commonly be unwilling to pay to solve the root cause of an Oracle performance problem. Managers are driven by cost savings and they are extremely averse to taking risks.

For example, instead of paying $100,000 to tune 1,000 SQL statements, the manager may instead spend $50,000 to move poor SQL to a faster server.

Embarrassed Management

Management may not want to publicly acknowledge that their "bargain" Oracle application was poorly designed. Even if the DBA proves that the Oracle schema needs a total reconstruction, the manager may not be willing to expose their poor judgment.

Embarrassed Vendors

Most vendor packages are designed with extremely generic SQL so that they can be easily ported to a variety of database platforms such as SQL Server, MySQL, and DB2, and they rarely make customization for Oracle-centric performance. Worst of all, most vendors do not like being told that their Oracle database layer needs to be tuned.

Vendors control the schema structures and the application layers. Even if a user finds sub-optimal SQL statements, they often cannot access the SQL source code in order to tune it.

These quirky vendor packages are the primary reason that Oracle offers specialized features such as optimizer plan stability (in the form of stored outlines) and the new Oracle10g SQL Profiles feature. In fact, Oracle has a wealth of tools for tuning vendor applications when the source code cannot be altered.

Emergency Oracle Support

When an Oracle performance problem cripples a mission-critical database, the DBA always gets the blame. The DBA is under great pressure during a database emergency and is always the target of everyone's attention. During these times of intense stress, the DBA may not have time for an elegant solution.

Testing a hypothesis on a large running database is like trying to tune a car while it's flying down the freeway at 75 miles per hour. It is impossible to reproduce the conditions of a complex performance breakdown, so the emergency support DBA must depend on experience and silver bullets to guide their plan of action.

21st Century Technology and Silver Bullets

The new super-cheap 32-way and 64-way Oracle data servers are causing massive server consolidation. This will have a huge effect on the way that Oracle DBAs tune their databases.

This new era of mainframe computing has forever changed the economics of the IT shop as hardware costs constantly fall while the costs of skilled computer professionals continue to rise (Figure 1.1).

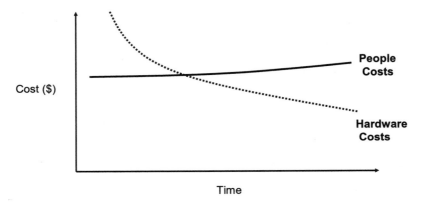

Figure 1.1: *The changing dynamics of human and hardware costs.*

In short, this shift in costs means that hardware has become a cheaper asset than the time of the Oracle professional. For example, when the schema design is sub-optimal, even materialized views may fail to correct the performance issues. In many cases, IT management does not want to hear about a need for an expensive re-design of the database for several reasons:

- **Fear of Blame** - No manager wants to admit that a poor database design was implemented under their watch.

- **High Downtime** - The time required to implement a table re-design can mean days of database downtime.

- **High Cost** - If the original implementation of the poor database costs $200k, the chance that management will spend the money all over again to re-design the system is very small.

The sad reality of server consolidation is that thousands of mediocre Oracle DBAs will lose their jobs to this trend.

The best DBAs will continue to find jobs, but neophyte Oracle DBAs who were used for the repetitive tasks of installing upgrades on hundreds of small servers will be displaced. This is especially true for shops undergoing server consolidation where 30 Oracle instances, each running on its own small server, may all be placed on a single mega-server.

Code Depot Username = reader, Password = ranger

So, what does this shifting dynamic mean to IT management? The following section outlines how Oracle DBAs are limited in their ability to tune their databases and how the shift in technology is going to change their job roles.

The Limitations of the DBA

There are many database problem areas that are beyond the scope of the Oracle DBA's control, and this can be very frustrating. The following is a short list of Oracle problems that the DBA may be prohibited from fixing:

- Poorly designed application or schema

- Inefficient PL/SQL within the application

- Excessive Transparent Network Substrate (TNS) calls within the application

- Dynamic SQL

- SQL without host variables

- Poorly-formed SQL statements

- Sub-optimal server kernel parms

So, do these bindings mean that the Oracle DBA is powerless to tune their databases? No, of course is doesn't. The DBA has a wealth of tuning tools at their disposal and many of these tools can have a positive effect on an entire database. The silver bullets allow for the tuning of many performance issues when the code cannot be changed directly:

- **Materialized Views** - Allows the DBA to fix bad schema normalization by pre-joining tables and pre-summarizing data values. Best of all, Oracle's materialized views (MV) feature uses Oracle replication to allow the DBA to pre-summarize and pre-join tables.

- **Indexes** - One of the best silver bullets, adding missing indexes or improving index selectivity with function-based indexes, can improve the efficiency of thousands of SQL statements.

- **Instance Parameters** - There are hundred of *init.ora* parameters that can have a huge effect on the performance of an Oracle database.

- **Object Parameters** - Internal table parameters such as *freelists, pctfree* and *pctused* can relieve contention within the I/O subsystem.

- **Tablespace Parameters** -New tablespace features such as Locally-Managed Tablespaces (LMT), Automatic Segment Space Management (bitmap freelists), and read-only tablespace can have a huge effect in reducing physical disk I/O on an Oracle database.

- **Table Structures** - The correct use of Index-Organized Tables (IOT) and table clusters can greatly reduce both Logical I/O (LIO) and Physical I/O (PIO) by grouping related data rows together in adjacent data blocks.

- **Segment Structures** - Controlling the block sizes for specific tablespaces can help reduce stress on the Oracle database by making more efficient use of expensive RAM data buffers.

- **Faster Hardware** - Once a database is fully-tuned, faster CPU and solid-state disk (RAM-SAN) can improve the throughput of the Oracle database.

These are the main focal areas of the use of silver bullets that will be examined in this book.

Managers often resist expensive or time-consuming solutions.

The Foundation of Oracle Silver Bullets

While the automated features of Oracle10g AMM, ASM, and automatic query re-write simplify the role of the Oracle DBA, savvy Oracle10g DBAs can now leverage other advanced Oracle 10g silver bullets to get super-fast performance:

- **Automated Workload Repository (AWR)** - The AWR is a critical component for data warehouse predictive tools such as the *dbms_advisor* package. AWR allows the DBA to run time-series reports of SQL access paths and intelligently create the most efficient materialized views for their warehouse. The AWR provides a time-series component of warehouse tuning that is critical for the identification of materialized views and holistic warehouse tuning. The most important data warehouse tracking with AWR includes tracking large-table full-table scans, multi-block reads, hash joins, and tracking RAM usage within the *pga_aggregate_target* region.

- **Multiple Blocksizes** - Multiple blocksizes can greatly reduce logical and physical I/O for objects that are accessed via range scans and Oracle objects that are accessed via multi-block reads, full-table, or full-index scans can be segregated into a larger blocksize to reduce I/O.

- **STAR Query Optimization** - The Oracle 10g STAR Query execution plan make it easy to make complex DSS queries run at super-fast speeds.

- **Multi-Level Partitioning of Tables and Indexes** - Oracle now has multi-level intelligent partitioning methods that allow Oracle to store data in a precise scheme. By controlling where data is stored on disk, Oracle10g SQL can reduce the disk I/O required to service any query.

- **Asynchronous Change Data Capture** - Change Data Capture allows incremental extraction, so only data that has changed can be extracted easily. For example, if a data warehouse extracts data from an operational system on a weekly basis, the data warehouse extracts only the data that has changed since the last extraction. In other words, it only takes the data that has been modified in the past seven days.

- **Oracle Streams** - Streams-based feed mechanisms can capture the necessary data changes from the operational database and send them to the destination data warehouse. The use of redo information by the Streams Capture process avoids unnecessary overhead on the production database.

- **Read-Only Tablespaces** - If a DBA has a time-series warehouse in which information eventually becomes static, using tablespace partitions and marking the older tablespaces as read-only can greatly improve performance. When a tablespace is marked as read-only, Oracle can bypass this read consistency mechanism, reducing overhead and resulting in faster throughput.

- **Automatic Storage Management (ASM)** - This revolutionary new method for managing the disk I/O subsystem removes the tedious and time consuming chore of I/O load balancing and disk management. With Oracle10g ASM, all disks can be logically clustered together into disk groups, and data files can be spread across all devices using the Oracle10g SAME (Stripe And Mirror Everywhere) standard. By making the disk back-end a JBOD (Just a Bunch of Disks), Oracle10g manages this critical aspect of the data warehouse.

- **Advanced Data Buffer Management** - Using Oracle 10g's multiple block sizes and KEEP pool, warehouse objects can be preassigned to separate data buffers and ensure that the working set of frequently referenced data is always cached.

Small, frequently referenced dimension tables should be cached using the Oracle 10g KEEP pool.

These are just a few examples of the silver bullets that will be presented in more detail later in this book. The next area that requires attention is Oracle emergency support and how holistic techniques can be used to quickly repair an ailing Oracle database.

Silver Bullets and Emergency Oracle Tuning

Huge stress levels and late night hours are an inevitable part of life for an emergency support DBA. Most of the databases will be unfamiliar and the DBA will only have a few minutes to assess the problem and create a plan to quickly relieve the bottleneck.

Only when the easy remedies have failed is the emergency support DBA called in. When a production database is in crisis, minimizing downtime is critical.

During this kind of crisis, cost is not an issue. The clients demand quick fixes, and this often requires unconventional methods.

These methods are usually driven by a client that may not appreciate the long-term benefits of a thoroughly devised fix for the root cause of the problem. Therefore, the emergency DBA is required to use every weapon in their arsenal to get the client running as soon as possible. This arsenal of stopgap remedies is often neither elegant nor comprehensive.

Functioning as an emergency Oracle support DBA can be great fun for the adrenaline junky. This kind of support often requires a unique set of techniques:

- **Fix the Symptom First** - The root cause can always be addressed later.

- **Time is Critical** - When a quick fix is required, instance-wide adjustments are often the best hope.

- **Be Creative** - Traditional time consuming tuning methods do not apply in an emergency.

Once the silver bullets have done their job and minimized the bottlenecks, the Emergency Oracle support DBA can only hope that the client will dedicate resources to the identification and long-term correction of the root cause of the problem.

Conclusion

This chapter has been an overview of Oracle silver bullets and how they are used in practice. The main points of this chapter include:

- **Management is Driven by Costs** - Oracle managers may not always choose the best tuning solution, especially if it involves risk, delay and high costs. Instead they often choose silver bullet approaches like Materialized Views and faster hardware.

- **Know the Bullets** - The most common silver bullets for the Oracle DBA are *init.ora* parameters, building indexes, especially function-based indexes, and using Materialized views.

- **Silver Bullets Come in Many Forms** - There are a large number of silver bullets that can be applied to Oracle including SGA bullets, instance bullets, optimizer bullets and hardware bullets.

- **Emergencies are Different** - In a crisis, the luxury of a detailed investigation and test plan is not allowed. The DBA must be ready to react quickly with powerful tools that can adjust Oracle and relieve the bottleneck.

Before details on specific silver bullets are presented, a quick look at how the job role of the DBA has been changing over the past decade is in order. The information in the next chapter will include how this affects the DBA's approach to optimization.

The Oracle DBA of the 21st Century

"I want a private office, a secretary and a company car."

What was Old is New Again

It is ironic that the old mainframe architectures of the 1970's and 1980's are now brand new again. Back in the days of "data processing," it was not uncommon for a single server to host more than a dozen databases.

The advent of the super-inexpensive Oracle servers is leading the way back to server consolidation. There was nothing inherently wrong with a centralized server environment, and in many ways it was superior to the distributed client-server architectures of the 1990's.

When companies first started to leave the mainframe environment, it was not because there were particular benefits to having a number of tiny servers. Instead, it was a pure economic decision based on the low cost of the UNIX-based minicomputers of the day.

These minicomputers of the 1980's could be purchased for as little as $30k which was a bargain when compared to the 3 million dollar cost of a mainframe. As minicomputers evolved into the UNIX-centric Oracle servers of the 1990's, some shops found themselves with hundreds of servers, one for each Oracle database.

 In fact, the migration away from the mainframe was a nightmare for the Oracle DBA. Instead of a single server to manage, the DBA had dozens or even hundreds of servers, each with its own copy of the Oracle software.

The 1990's was the age of *"client-server computing,"* where multi-tiered applications were constructed with dozens of small servers. Systems might have been comprised of a Web server layer, an application server layer, and a database layer, each with dozens of individual servers.

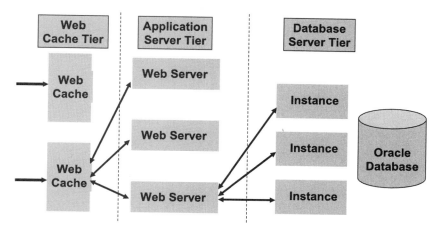

Figure 2.1: *The multi-server Oracle architectures of the 1990's.*

The example in Figure 2.1 shows a multi-server architecture that employs Oracle Real Application Clusters (RAC) which is a processing architecture that allows multiple Oracle instances on separate servers that access a common Oracle database.

The Ancient Oracle Architecture

One of the issues associated with the ancient single-server Oracle systems was the deliberate over-allocation of computing resources.

Each system would experience periodic processing spikes, and each server had to be equipped with additional resources to accommodate the irregular frequency of the demands of various applications. This led to a condition in which Oracle servers had unused CPU and RAM resources that could not be easily shared.

The ancient client-server Oracle paradigm presented many serious problems for the Oracle DBA:

- **High Expense** - In large enterprise data centers with many servers and many instances, hardware resources must be deliberately over-allocated in order to accommodate the sporadic peaks in CPU and RAM resources.

- **High Waste** - Since each Oracle instance resides on a separate single server, there is a significant duplication of work which results in sub-optimal utilization of RAM and CPU resources.

- **Very Time Consuming for the Oracle DBA** - In many large Oracle shops, a "shuffle" occurs when a database outgrows its server. When a new server is purchased, the Oracle database is moved to the new server, leaving the older server to accept yet another smaller Oracle database. This shuffling consumes considerable time and attention from the DBA.

This waste and high DBA overhead has lead IT managers to recognize the benefits of a centralized server environment, and there is now resurgence in popularity of large monolithic servers for bigger Oracle shops. There is also a rapid depreciation rate for servers which also contributed to the move toward server consolidation. For example, three year-old Oracle servers that cost over $100k new are now worth less than $5k.

These new Oracle server mainframes may contain 16, 32, or even 64 CPUs and have processing capabilities that dwarf the traditional mainframe ancestors of the 1980's. There are those who argue that it is not a good idea to throw everything into a single server because it introduces a single point of failure. Even Oracle Corporation says that it is not a good idea to place all of the proverbial eggs in one basket, and therefore, advocates the grid approach in Oracle10g.

Many of these concerns are unfounded. In reality, these large systems have redundant everything, and with the use of Oracle Streams for replication at different geographical locations, they are virtually unstoppable.

In the new server architectures, everything from disk, CPU, RAM, and internal busses are fully fault tolerant and redundant which makes the monolithic approach appealing to large corporations for the following reasons:

- **Lower Costs** - Monolithic servers are extremely good at sharing computing resources between applications, making grid computing unnecessary.

- **Lower Oracle DBA Maintenance** - Instead of maintaining 30 copies or more of Oracle and the OS, DBA's only need to manage a single copy.

Cost savings aside, there are other compelling reasons to consolidate Oracle instances onto a single server. In the past, with dozens of Oracle DBA staff, important tasks were often overlooked because of an "It's not my job" mentality. The evolving technology is changing all of this, and the 21st Century DBA will have more overall responsibility for the whole operation of their Oracle database:

- **Centralized DBA Management** - A single server means a single copy of the Oracle software. Plus, the operating system controls resource allocation and the server will automatically balance the demands of many Oracle instances for processing cycles and RAM resources. Of course, the Oracle DBA still maintains control and can dedicate Oracle instances to a single CPU (processor affinity) or adjust the CPU dispatching priority (the UNIX "nice" command) of important Oracle tasks.

- **Transparent High Availability** - If a CPU fails, the monolithic server can re-assign the processing without interruption. This is a more affordable and far simpler solution than RAC or Oracle9i Data Guard, either of which requires duplicate servers.

- **Reduced DBA Workload** - By consolidating server resources, the DBA has fewer servers to manage and need not be concerned with outgrowing their server.

So, what does this mean to the Oracle DBA? Clearly, less time will be spent installing and maintaining multiple copies of Oracle, and this will free-up time for the DBA to pursue more advanced tasks such as SQL tuning and database performance optimization.

The fact that computing resources are displacing human resources has a profound impact of the job duties of the Oracle DBA. Oracle instances are becoming consolidated onto large servers with 32 and 64 CPUs, and as a result, less DBA staff is required. At the same time, DBA responsibilities are expanding as the surviving DBA's need to manage schema design, security, and other mission-critical data management tasks.

The surviving Oracle DBA's will find themselves with many new job roles. They will be relieved of the tedium of applying patches to multiple servers, constantly re-allocating server resources, and tuning many servers. The DBA job role will become far more demanding, and many companies are already starting to view the DBA as a technical management position, encompassing far more responsibility than the traditional DBA.

As Oracle professionals are relieved of the tedious, well-structured and repetitive tasks of patch application monitoring and tuning, the DBA is free to pursue more important data management tasks.

The expense of over-allocated multiple server resources is not the only reason for the move toward server consolidation. There will be a dramatic savings in human resources and an increase of overall performance because:

- **High Scalability** - Large, single servers provide on-demand resource allocation by sharing CPU and RAM between many resources.

- **Fewer IT Staff** - There are less human resources required to manage a single server.

- **High Performance** - The SMP architecture allows for on-demand allocation of RAM and CPU resources for all Oracle instances.

Conclusion

A migration to a large, single Oracle server allows the support of dozens of Oracle instances, each with complete access to the shared CPU and RAM resources. Best of all, the resource allocation is automatic and reliable, and requires no human intervention.

This massive server consolidation effort is a silver bullet that is presented in more detail in Chapter 11, Oracle Hardware Silver Bullets. The next chapter presents detailed information on proactive Oracle tuning and how it lends itself to silver bullet applications.

Proactive Tuning and Silver Bullets

CHAPTER

3

The Many Faces of Oracle Databases

Oracle databases are extremely dynamic and constantly changing. The database may be constrained by memory in one instant and I/O the next. Nobody can deny that tuning a constantly changing environment is a challenge.

This chapter will cover the concept of time-series tuning where metrics are tracked over time, and holistic adjustments are used to keep Oracle running at peak performance. This chapter will cover following topics, all from a proactive, time-series perspective:

- The proactive tuning approach

- Bottleneck analysis

- External bottlenecks

- Instance Tuning

- Object Tuning

- SQL tuning

Major sections of this book have been devoted to silver bullets for these issues; however, a quick high-level look at the main issues in this chapter is included. Oracle tuning is a complex endeavor.

Even the automated tuning tools within Oracle are not always sufficient to tune large, complex Oracle databases and a proactive tuning approach must be combined with proven Oracle silver bullets.

There are many approaches to tuning, and while every method seeks to remedy a bottleneck, each approach is very different.

The next step is to gather information on the proactive tuning approach and how time-series tuning is a great silver bullet for a DBA's arsenal of tools.

The Proactive Tuning Approach

With the incorporation of the tuning tool known as STATSPACK utility into the Oracle database kernel as a new feature called Automated Workload Repository (AWR), Oracle tuning professionals were given a data repository that allows the leisurely analysis of Oracle performance statistics and trends over time.

The AWR allows DBAs to devise a general tuning strategy that addresses different kinds of processing that can take place within the Oracle application and apply broad brush silver bullets to their Oracle database.

This approach is known as proactive tuning. In proactive tuning, the Oracle DBA's goal is to tune the database by finding the optimal global parameters and settings that will maximize Oracle throughput at any given point in time. By using a proactive approach to Oracle tuning, the Oracle DBA can ensure that the database is optimally tuned for the type of processing that is demanded of it.

The dynamic SGA feature of Oracle, which was initiated in Oracle9i, allows AWR information to be used for dynamic SGA reconfiguration. For example, if the AWR shows that the demands on the shared pool become very high between 1:00 pm and 2:00 pm, the DBA could trigger a dynamic increase of the *shared_pool_size* parameter during this time period.

AWR tables are quite simple. Whenever a snapshot is requested, Oracle interrogates the in-memory *v$* structures and places the information in the appropriate Oracle *dba_hist* tables.

Having AWR information captured over periods of time gives the DBA the opportunity to accurately model an optimal performance plan for the database.

Trend Analysis and Oracle Silver Bullets

Savvy Oracle tuning professionals know that reactive tuning has limited value and the real key to success is time-series tuning.

Third-party tools such as the STATSPACK Viewer and the Workload Interface Statistical Engine (WISE) capture Oracle

AWR and STATSPACK data easily and allow the DBA to visualize the data aggregated by averages for day-of-the-week and hour-of-the day.

The WISE tool is inexpensive at $9.95 for Standard Edition and $199 for Enterprise Edition, and it provides a time-saving tool for plotting Oracle performance trends and repeating signatures for performance metrics (www.wise-oracle.com). Moreover, Oracle DBA's have the unique ability to visually represent AWR information using the WISE tool by drawing on numerous reports run against *dba_hist* tables. The WISE tool provides DBA's with a convenient framework to work with AWR performance data and produce charts to support proactive tuning. Throughout the remainder of this book, information will be presented on how a graphics tool like WISE can be used to facilitate proactive tuning and help the DBA find silver bullets. The knowledge of aggregated average values by day-of-the-week and hour-of-the-day can assist in the proper configuration of Oracle.

Tuning a Constantly Changing Database

Oracle has recognized that it is impossible to create a one-size-fits-all approach to tuning a database. The database is in a constant state of flux and the ideal tuning approach must react to changes in processing demands, reallocating resources in real time.

To the small business user, Oracle10g automation regulates data file and storage management, changes the sizes of the SGA regions and reactively self-tunes performance issues. Is a reactive approach enough? It is often too-late to make changes after the end user has suffered from poor response time. The real goal of Oracle tuning is to anticipate changes in processing and reallocate resources just-in-time.

Does Oracle Possess Psychic Abilities?

Just as the name implies, Oracle can indeed predict the future, sometimes with remarkable accuracy. Instead of relying on mystic or spiritual sources, Oracle can learn from experience, and use this experience to predict the future.

This is the core of time-series tuning. Almost all Oracle databases experience repeating patterns of usage, predictable by hour-of-the-day and day-of-the-week. Once a statistically valid pattern of events has been detected, the DBA can schedule a reconfiguration, just-in-time to meet the change in requirements and before the end user experiences degradation in response time.

Trend-Based Oracle Reconfiguration

One common approach to trend-based reconfiguration is to use STATSPACK or AWR historical data to proactively reconfigure the database. A good analogy is just-in-time manufacturing, where parts appear on the plant floor just as they are needed for assembly. Oracle9i enables the DBA to anticipate processing needs and regularly schedule appropriate intervention, insuring that SGA resources are delivered just-in-time for processing tasks.

For those who would like to investigate STATSPACK and AWR features and abilities at a deeper level, two informative books are available from Oracle Press and a third will be published by Rampant TechPress later in 2005:

- *Oracle High-performance Tuning with STATSPACK*
  Oracle Press, by Donald K. Burleson.

- *Oracle9i High-performance Tuning with STATSPACK*
  Oracle Press, by Donald K. Burleson.

- *Oracle Tuning - Oracle Time-Series Optimization with the Automatic Workload Repository*
  Rampant TechPress, by Alexey Danchenkov and Donald K. Burleson.

The wide range of techniques and options available for trend identification using STATSPACK and AWR are beyond the scope of this book.

It is easy to schedule tasks that change the RAM memory configuration as the processing needs change on a UNIX platform. For example, it is common for Oracle databases to operate in Online Transaction Processing (OLTP) mode during normal work hours and perform the database services memory intensive batch reports at night. An OLTP database requires a large *db_cache_size* value. Memory intensive batch tasks require additional RAM in the *pga_aggregate_target* parameter.

The UNIX scripts given below can be used to reconfigure the SGA between the OLTP and DSS without stopping the instance. The example assumes an isolated Oracle server with 8 gigabytes of RAM, with 10 percent of RAM reserved for UNIX overhead, leaving 7.2 gigabytes for Oracle and Oracle connections. The scripts are intended either for HP-UX or Solaris and accept the $ORACLE_SID as an argument.

This *dss_config.ksh* script is scheduled to run at 6:00 p.m. each evening in order to reconfigure Oracle for the memory-intensive batch tasks.

dss_config.ksh

```
-- ****************************************************
-- Copyright © 2005 by Rampant TechPress
-- This script is free for non-commercial purposes
-- with no warranties.  Use at your own risk.
--
-- To license this script for a commercial purpose,
```

```
-- contact info@rampant.cc
-- *********************************************

#!/bin/ksh

# First, we must set the environment . . . .
ORACLE_SID=$1
export ORACLE_SID
ORACLE_HOME=`cat /etc/oratab|grep ^$ORACLE_SID:|cut -f2 -d':'`
#ORACLE_HOME=`cat /var/opt/oracle/oratab|grep ^$ORACLE_SID:|cut -f2
-d':'`
export ORACLE_HOME
PATH=$ORACLE_HOME/bin:$PATH
export PATH

$ORACLE_HOME/bin/sqlplus -s /nologin<<!
connect system/manager as sysdba;
alter system set db_cache_size=1500m;
alter system set shared_pool_size=500m;
alter system set pga_aggregate_target=4000m;
exit
!
```

The script below is scheduled to run at 6:00 a.m. each morning to reconfigure Oracle for the OLTP usage during the day.

oltp_config.ksh

```
-- *********************************************
-- Copyright © 2005 by Rampant TechPress
-- This script is free for non-commercial purposes
-- with no warranties.  Use at your own risk.
--
-- To license this script for a commercial purpose,
-- contact info@rampant.cc
-- *********************************************

#!/bin/ksh

# First, we must set the environment . . . .
ORACLE_SID=$1
export ORACLE_SID
ORACLE_HOME=`cat /etc/oratab|grep ^$ORACLE_SID:|cut -f2 -d':'`
#ORACLE_HOME=`cat /var/opt/oracle/oratab|grep ^$ORACLE_SID:|cut -f2
-d':'`
export ORACLE_HOME
PATH=$ORACLE_HOME/bin:$PATH
export PATH

$ORACLE_HOME/bin/sqlplus -s /nologin<<!
connect system/manager as sysdba;
```

```
alter system set db_cache_size=4000m;
alter system set shared_pool_size=500m;
alter system set pga_aggregate_target=1500m;

exit
!
```

The *dbms_job* and *dbms_schedule* packages can also be used to schedule the reconfigurations.

It should now be apparent that the Oracle DBA can develop spy routines to constantly monitor the processing demands on the database and issue the *alter system* commands to dynamically respond to these conditions. It is only through this proactive monitoring and adjustment that the DBA can free up their time for other critical job duties.

Self-Tuning with Silver Bullets

The Oracle DBA can adjust the RAM configuration according to the types of processing that is happening within the SGA. Generally, queries against the *v$* structures and STATSPACK will pinpoint those times when Oracle connections change their processing characteristics. There are three approaches to automated tuning:

- **Normal Scheduled Reconfiguration** – This is a bimodal instance that performs OLTP and DSS during regular hours will benefit from a scheduled task to reconfigure the SGA and PGA.

- **Trend-Based Dynamic Reconfiguration** -STATSPACK can be used to predict those times when the processing characteristics change and use the *dbms_job* package to fire ad-hoc SGA and PGA changes.

- **Dynamic Reconfiguration** - Just as Oracle9i dynamically redistributes RAM memory for tasks within the *pga_aggregate_target* region, the Oracle DBA can write scripts that take RAM from an under-utilized area and reallocate these RAM pages to another RAM area.

The next section outlines how Oracle may evolve to allow super-fast dynamic reconfiguration.

Capturing Time-Series Metrics

The Oracle DBA has a wealth of Oracle performance information at their fingertips, with more than 100 new dynamic performance tables stored in the Automatic Workload Repository (AWR).

These AWR tables feed data to the totally reworked Enterprise Manager (EM) to produce stunning time-series displays. AWR data is used by the Automatic Database Diagnostic Monitor (ADDM) and the SQL Tuning Advisor or by using the *dbms_sqltune* package to make intelligent performance recommendations.

Instead of running complex scripts to track database performance over time, the Oracle10g DBA now has detailed time-series performance data immediately available for detailed analysis. These industrial strength AWR tables are a blessing for the Oracle tuning DBA. Oracle10g has new DBMS packages, such as the *dbms_sqltune and dbms_mview.explain_rewrite* packages, that read the *wrh$* tables and carry out sophisticated performance analysis. While not artificial intelligence in the truest sense, these sophisticated tools help simplify the complex task of Oracle tuning.

Trend Identification with the AWR

Once the creation of simple *dba_hist* queries has been mastered, the next step is to move on to examine trend identification with the AWR views. The Oracle professional knows that aggregating important performance metrics over time (day-of-the-week and hour-of-the-day) allows them to see performance signatures that may otherwise remain hidden. These signatures are extremely important for proactive tuning because they show regularly occurring changes in processing demands. This knowledge allows for the anticipation of upcoming changes in order to reconfigure Oracle just-in-time to meet the changes.

The following is a simple example. This example utilizes a report called *rpt_sysstat_hr_10g.sql* that will show the signature for any Oracle system statistic, averaged by hour of the day.

rpt_sysstat_hr_10g.sql

```
--  *************************************************
--  Copyright © 2005 by Rampant TechPress
--  This script is free for non-commercial purposes
--  with no warranties.  Use at your own risk.
--
--  To license this script for a commercial purpose,
--  contact info@rampant.cc
--  *************************************************

prompt
prompt
prompt  This will query the dba_hist_sysstat view to
prompt  display average values by hour of the day
prompt

set pages 999

break on snap_time skip 2

accept stat_name char prompt 'Enter Statistics Name:  ';

col snap_time    format a19
col avg_value    format 999,999,999

select
```

```
   to_char(begin_interval_time,'hh24')  snap_time,
   avg(value)                           avg_value
from
   dba_hist_sysstat
  natural join
   dba_hist_snapshot
where
   stat_name = '&stat_name'
group by
   to_char(begin_interval_time,'hh24')
order by
   to_char(begin_interval_time,'hh24')
;
```

The output contains an average for every hour of the day. Figure 3.1 below shows a graphical representation of the data after it has been pasted into an MS Excel spreadsheet and plotted with the Excel chart wizard.

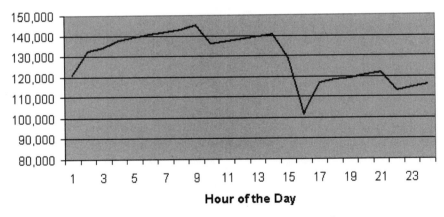

Figure 3.1: *An hourly Signature can show hidden trends.*

Open source products such as RRDtool and WISE can also be used to automate the plotting of data from the AWR and ASH as shown in Figure 3.2.

The WISE tool is a great way to quickly plot Oracle time series data and gather signatures for Oracle metrics. Below is an example of how the WISE tool displays this data. (See www.wise-oracle.com for details)

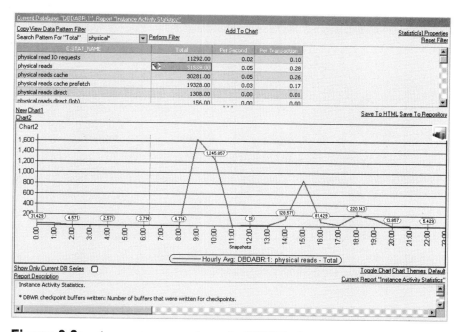

Figure 3.2: *Aggregate output from the WISE viewer.*

The same types of reports aggregated by day-of-the week can be created so the DBA can see ongoing daily trends. Over long periods of time, almost all Oracle databases will develop distinct signatures that reflect the regular daily processing patterns of the end user community.

The following script, *rpt_sysstat_dy_10g.sql,* will accept any of the values from *dba_hist_sysstat* and plot the average values by hour of the day.

```
-- **************************************************
-- Copyright © 2005 by Rampant TechPress
-- This script is free for non-commercial purposes
-- with no warranties.  Use at your own risk.
--
-- To license this script for a commercial purpose,
-- contact info@rampant.cc
-- **************************************************

prompt
prompt  This will query the dba_hist_sysstat view to display
prompt  average values by day-of-the-week
prompt

set pages 999

accept stat_name char prompt 'Enter Statistic Name:  ';


col snap_time     format a19
col avg_value     format 999,999,999

select
   to_char(begin_interval_time,'day')    snap_time,
   avg(value)                            avg_value
from
   dba_hist_sysstat
natural join
   dba_hist_snapshot
where
   stat_name = '&stat_name'
group by
   to_char(begin_interval_time,'day')
order by
   decode(
   to_char(begin_interval_time,'day'),
    'sunday',1,
    'monday',2,
    'tuesday',3,
    'wednesday',4,
    'thursday',5,
    'friday',6,
    'saturday',7
   )
;
```

The following is the output from this script:

```
SQL> @rpt_sysstat_dy_10g

This will query the dba_hist_sysstat view to display
average values by day-of-the-week

Enter Statistics Name:  physical reads

SNAP_TIME                    AVG_VALUE
------------------    ------------
sunday                     190,185
monday                     135,749
tuesday                     83,313
wednesday                  139,627
thursday                   105,815
friday                     107,250
saturday                   154,279
```

These results show an average for every day of the week.

If resource issues can be predicted before they occur, the DBA can plan ahead and reallocate resources such as SGA regions or change the configuration of Oracle through the dynamic parameters. The *dbms_scheduler* package can then be used to morph the Oracle instance just-in-time to accommodate the processing need.

Conclusion

This chapter has been an overview of the proactive holistic approach to Oracle tuning. At this point, it should be apparent that the only way to achieve effective Oracle tuning over time is to develop a strategy for monitoring performance trends. The main points of this chapter include:

- **Always Tune the System First** - It can be foolhardy to start tuning individual applications or SQL statements until the instance is optimized.

- **Use a Broad Brush** - There are many silver bullet parameters and settings that can improve the performance of an entire application.

- **Tune to a Baseline** - Reactive "what's happening now" approaches rarely succeed. DBA's must endeavor to use STATSPACK or the AWR to apply time-series approaches to their databases.

- **Go Top-Down** - Global tuning is performed through a review of the instance configuration such as initialization parameters and CBO statistics. After the review, the challenge becomes choosing the best overall settings. Detailed tuning is performed by tuning the individual SQL statements. Ongoing tuning is the process of adjusting the dynamic Oracle parameters in anticipation of changes in processing profiles.

Now that the basic ideas behind proactive holistic Oracle tuning have been examined, the next step is to investigate how a DBA can perform a hierarchical Oracle performance review.

The Silver Bullet Hierarchy

Oracle databases can go bad very quickly

The Top-Down Approach to Silver Bullets

The following is a top-down approach to Oracle tuning that has been very successful for tuning large and highly active Oracle systems. It is a top-down approach that starts with the review of the external and instance bottlenecks and then the application, moving from global to specific. The final step is the application of Oracle silver bullet techniques to the instance and objects. This hierarchy is shown in Figure 4.1.

These tuning steps generally include:

- **Review of the External Environment** – This consists of a review of the server, disk and network environment to ascertain when hardware components are overly stressed.

- **Review Instance Performance Metrics** – This consists of a review of the top wait events within AWR over a period of time to understand the overall instance performance.

- **Perform Instance Tuning** – This consists of the adjustment of system wide parameters that affect the behavior of the system. Since any database is in a constant state of flux, it is critical to identify the best overall setting for each of Oracle's 250+ initialization parameters.

- **Perform Object Tuning** – This consists of a review of specific wait events that are closely tied to data files, tablespaces, tables and indexes. The source of the stress is examined, and the object characteristics are then adjusted in order to remove the bottleneck.

- **SQL Tuning** - This is the most time intensive of the tuning tasks. The *dba_hist* views are used to extract sub-optimal SQL by way of the identification of sub-optimal table join order, unnecessary large-table full-table scans, or inefficient execution plans. The SQL is then tuned manually by using hints or the Oracle10g SQL Tuning Advisor to create SQL Profiles for tuning the statements.

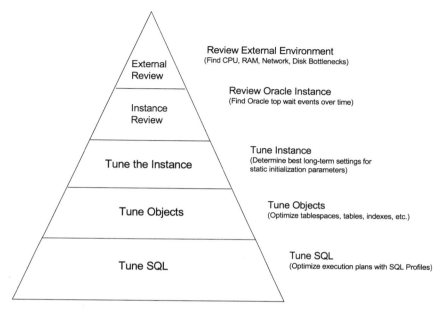

Figure 4.1: *The Oracle Tuning Hierarchy.*

The following is a quick overview of these steps. For more detailed information, Rampant TechPress will be publishing a book on Oracle Tuning in 2005. An investigation of the external environmental review is a good starting point.

External Hardware Performance Review

Oracle does not run in a vacuum. The performance of Oracle databases depends heavily on external considerations, namely the Oracle server, disk and network. The first tasks when tuning a database are to identify the external bottleneck conditions, which may include:

- **CPU Bottleneck** - The number of CPU cycles available can slow down SQL. Whenever the run queue exceeds the number of CPUs on the Oracle server in the absence of high idle time, the system is CPU-bound. CPU consumption can be reduced by tuning SQL or reducing library cache contention; however, a CPU shortage may indicate a need to add more, or faster, processors to the Oracle server.

- **RAM Bottleneck** - The amount of available RAM memory for Oracle can affect the performance of SQL, especially in the data buffers and in-memory sorts.

- **Network Bottleneck** - Large amounts of Oracle*Net traffic contribute to slow SQL performance.

- **Disk Bottleneck** - Disk bottlenecks can be identified by the fact that updates are slow due to RAID5 and channel contention.

There are several simple items to monitor when checking the external Oracle environment:

- **CPU Run Queue Waits** - When the number of run queue waits exceeds the number of CPUs on the server, the server is experiencing a CPU shortage. The remedy is the addition of CPUs on the server or the disabling of high stress processing components such as Oracle Parallel Query.

- **RAM Page-Ins** - When RAM page-in operations combined with a prior increase in scan rate are indicated, the existing RAM memory has been exceeded and memory pages are moving in from the swap space on disk. The remedy is to add more RAM, reduce the size of the Oracle SGAs, or turn-on Oracle's multi-threaded server.

- **Disk Enqueues** - Enqueues on a disk device indicate that the read-write heads cannot move fast enough to keep up with data access requirements.

- **Network Latency** - Volume-related network latency may indicate either the need to tune the application to make fewer requests or a need for faster network hardware.

While it is easy to describe these external bottlenecks, it's not always easy to find them.

Finding Database Bottlenecks

Every Oracle database has at least one physical constraint, and it is not always disk. The best way to isolate the constraints in the system is to analyze the top five wait events for the database and look for external waits associated with disk, CPU and network.

The best way to see system-level wait summaries is to run the *awrrpt.sql* script from the $ORACLE_HOME/rdbms/admin directory.

This standard Oracle time-series report will show all performance aspects on the database during the specified time period, and most important of all, yield the top 5 timed events for the specific interval between AWR snapshots.

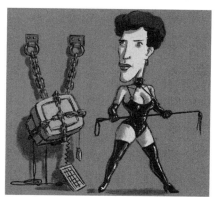

Oracle Bottlenecks are an onerous form of bondage

The script below, *wait_time_detail.sql*, compares the wait event values from *dba_hist_waitstat* and *dba_hist_active_sess_history*. This approach allows the identification of the exact objects that are experiencing wait events.

wait_time_detail.sql

```
--  ****************************************************
-- Copyright © 2005 by Rampant TechPress
-- This script is free for non-commercial purposes
-- with no warranties.  Use at your own risk.
--
-- To license this script for a commercial purpose,
-- contact info@rampant.cc
--  ****************************************************

set pages 999
set lines 80

break on snap_time skip 2

col snap_time      heading 'Snap|Time'    format a20
col file_name      heading 'File|Name'    format a40
col object_type    heading 'Object|Type'  format a10
col object_name    heading 'Object|Name'  format a20
col wait_count     heading 'Wait|Count'   format 999,999
col time           heading 'Time'         format 999,999

select
   to_char(begin_interval_time,'yyyy-mm-dd hh24:mi') snap_time,
--    file_name,
   object_type,
   object_name,
   wait_count,
   time
from
   dba_hist_waitstat              wait,
   dba_hist_snapshot              snap,
   dba_hist_active_sess_history   ash,
   dba_data_files                 df,
   dba_objects                    obj
where
   wait.snap_id = snap.snap_id
and
   wait.snap_id = ash.snap_id
and
   df.file_id = ash.current_file#
and
   obj.object_id = ash.current_obj#
and
   wait_count > 50
order by
   to_char(begin_interval_time,'yyyy-mm-dd hh24:mi'),
   file_name
;
```

This script enables joining into the *dba_data_files* view to get the file names associated with the wait event. This is a very powerful script that can be used to quickly drill-in to find the cause of specific waits. A sample output looks like:

```
SQL> @wait_time_detail
```

This will compare values from dba_hist_waitstat with detail information from dba_hist_active_sess_history.

Snap Time	Object Type	Object Name	Wait Count	Time
2004-02-28 01:00	TABLE	ORDOR	4,273	67
	INDEX	PK_CUST_ID	12,373	324
	INDEX	FK_CUST_NAME	3,883	17
	INDEX	PK_ITEM_ID	1,256	967
2004-02-29 03:00	TABLE	ITEM_DETAIL	83	69
2004-03-01 04:00	TABLE	ITEM_DETAIL	1,246	45
2004-03-01 21:00	TABLE	CUSTOMER_DET	4,381	354
	TABLE	IND_PART	117	15
2004-03-04 01:00	TABLE	MARVIN	41,273	16
	TABLE	FACTOTUM	2,827	43
	TABLE	DOW_KNOB	853	6
	TABLE	ITEM_DETAIL	57	331
	TABLE	HIST_ORD	4,337	176
	TABLE	TAB_HIST	127	66

Top wait events can also be quickly identified by using the Top Wait Events report in WISE as shown in Figure 4.2.

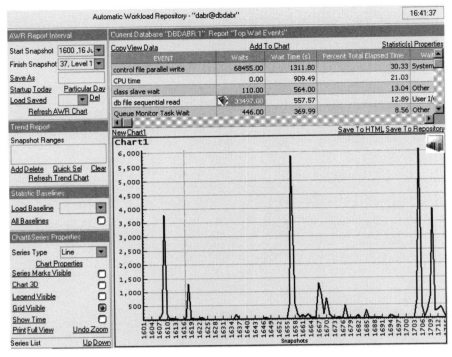

EVENT	Waits	Wait Time (s)	Percent Total Elapsed Time	Wait
control file parallel write	68455.00	1311.80	30.33	System
CPU time	0.00	909.49	21.03	
class slave wait	110.00	564.00	13.04	Other
db file sequential read	33497.00	557.57	12.89	User I/O
Queue Monitor Task Wait	446.00	369.99	8.56	Other

Figure 4.2: *Top Wait Events report in WISE.*

The following section presents information on finding I/O-related bottlenecks.

Disk Constrained Databases

In a disk-bound database, the majority of the wait time is spent accessing data blocks. This can be db file sequential read waits, which is usually index access, and db file scattered read waits, which is usually full-table scans as evidenced by the following AWR report section:

```
Top 5 Timed Events

                                                      % Total
Event                         Waits      Time(s)    Ela Time
--------------------------  -----------  ----------  --------
db file sequential read       2,598       7,146      48.54
db file scattered read       25,519       3,246      22.04
library cache load lock         673       1,363       9.26
CPU time                         44       1,154       7.83
log file parallel write      19,157         837       5.68
```

I/O bound databases can be tuned down by any number of holistic techniques including large data buffers with 64-bit Oracle, changing RAID levels on the disk and using high speed solid-state RAM-disk.

The *dba_hist_sqlstat* table is a great way to find disk bottlenecks. This view is very similar to the *v$sql* view, but it contains important SQL metrics for each snapshot. These include important delta (change) information on disk reads and buffer gets, as well as time-series delta information on application, I/O and concurrency wait times. The following is a script that queries this view for this performance information.

awr_sqlstat_deltas.sql

```
-- ********************************************************
-- Copyright © 2005 by Rampant TechPress
-- This script is free for non-commercial purposes
-- with no warranties.  Use at your own risk.
--
-- To license this script for a commercial purpose,
-- contact info@rampant.cc
-- ********************************************************

col c1 heading 'Begin|Interval|time'      format a8
col c2 heading 'SQL|ID'                    format a13
col c3 heading 'Exec|Delta'                format 9,999
col c4 heading 'Buffer|Gets|Delta'         format 9,999
col c5 heading 'Disk|Reads|Delta'          format 9,999
col c6 heading 'IO Wait|Delta'             format 9,999
col c7 heading 'Application|Wait|Delta'    format 9,999
col c8 heading 'Concurrency|Wait|Delta'    format 9,999


break on c1

select
```

```
    to_char(s.begin_interval_time,'mm-dd hh24')   c1,
    sql.sql_id                c2,
    sql.executions_delta      c3,
    sql.buffer_gets_delta     c4,
    sql.disk_reads_delta      c5,
    sql.iowait_delta          c6,
    sql.apwait_delta          c7,
    sql.ccwait_delta          c8
from
    dba_hist_sqlstat          sql,
    dba_hist_snapshot          s
where
    s.snap_id = sql.snap_id
order by
    c1,
    c2
;
```

The following is a sample of the output. This is very important because it shows the changes in SQL execution over time periods. For each snapshot period, the change in the number of times that the SQL was executed as well as important information about the performance of the statement is shown.

Begin Interval time	SQL ID	Exec Delta	Buffer Gets Delta	Disk Reads Delta	IO Wait Delta	Application Wait Delta	Concurrency Wait Delta
10-10 16	0sfgqjz5cs52w	24	72	12	0	3	0
	1784a4705pt01	1	685	6	0	17	0
	19rkm1wsf9axx	10	61	4	0	0	0
	1d5d88cnwxcw4	52	193	4	6	0	0
	1fvsn5j51ugz3	4	0	0	0	0	0
	1uym1vta995yb	1	102	0	0	0	0
	23yu0nncnp8m9	24	72	0	0	6	0
	298ppdduqr7wm	1	3	0	0	0	0
	2cpffmjm98pcm	4	12	0	0	0	0
	2prbzh4qfms7u	1	4,956	19	1	34	5
10-10 17	0sfgqjz5cs52w	30	90	1	0	0	0
	19rkm1wsf9axx	14	88	0	0	0	0
	1fvsn5j51ugz3	4	0	0	0	0	0
	1zcdwkknwdpgh	4	4	0	0	0	0
	23yu0nncnp8m9	30	91	0	0	0	5
	298ppdduqr7wm	1	3	0	0	0	0
	2cpffmjm98pcm	4	12	0	0	0	0

This report is especially useful because it allows tracking of the Logical I/O (buffer gets) vs. Physical I/O for each statement over time, thereby yielding important information about the behavior of the SQL statement.

This output gives a quick overview of the top SQL during any AWR snapshot period and shows how their behavior has changed since the last snapshot period. Detecting changes in the behavior of commonly executed SQL statements is the key to time-series SQL tuning.

As shown below, a WHERE clause can easily be added to the above script so that the I/O changes over time can be plotted:

awr_sqlstat_deltas_detail.sql

```
--  *************************************************
--  Copyright © 2005 by Rampant TechPress
--  This script is free for non-commercial purposes
--  with no warranties.  Use at your own risk.
--
--  To license this script for a commercial purpose,
--  contact info@rampant.cc
--  *************************************************

col c1  heading  'Begin|Interval|time'     format a8
col c2  heading  'Exec|Delta'              format 999,999
col c3  heading  'Buffer|Gets|Delta'       format 999,999
col c4  heading  'Disk|Reads|Delta'        format 9,999
col c5  heading  'IO Wait|Delta'           format 9,999
col c6  heading  'App|Wait|Delta'          format 9,999
col c7  heading  'Cncr|Wait|Delta'         format 9,999
col c8  heading  'CPU|Time|Delta'          format 999,999
col c9  heading  'Elpsd|Time|Delta'        format 999,999

accept sqlid prompt 'Enter SQL ID: '
ttitle 'time series execution for|&sqlid'
break on c1

select
  to_char(s.begin_interval_time,'mm-dd hh24')  c1,
  sql.executions_delta      c2,
  sql.buffer_gets_delta     c3,
  sql.disk_reads_delta      c4,
  sql.iowait_delta          c5,
  sql.apwait_delta          c6,
  sql.ccwait_delta          c7,
  sql.cpu_time_delta        c8,
  sql.elapsed_time_delta    c9
from
   dba_hist_sqlstat         sql,
   dba_hist_snapshot          s
where
```

```
    s.snap_id = sql.snap_id
and
    sql_id = '&sqlid'
order by
    c1
;
```

The output shows the changes to the execution of a frequently used SQL statement and how its behavior changes over time:

Begin Interval time	Exec Delta	Buffer Gets Delta	Disk Reads Delta	IO Wait Delta	App Wait Delta	Cncr Wait Delta	CPU Time Delta	Elpsd Time Delta
10-14 10	709	2,127	0	0	0	0	398,899	423,014
10-14 11	696	2,088	0	0	0	0	374,502	437,614
10-14 12	710	2,130	0	0	0	0	384,579	385,388
10-14 13	693	2,079	0	0	0	0	363,648	378,252
10-14 14	708	2,124	0	0	0	0	373,902	373,902
10-14 15	697	2,091	0	0	0	0	388,047	410,605
10-14 16	707	2,121	0	0	0	0	386,542	491,830
10-14 17	698	2,094	0	0	0	0	378,087	587,544
10-14 18	708	2,124	0	0	0	0	376,491	385,816
10-14 19	695	2,085	0	0	0	0	361,850	361,850
10-14 20	708	2,124	0	0	0	0	368,889	368,889
10-14 21	696	2,088	0	0	0	0	363,111	412,521
10-14 22	709	2,127	0	0	0	0	369,015	369,015
10-14 23	695	2,085	0	0	0	0	362,480	362,480
10-15 00	709	2,127	0	0	0	0	368,554	368,554
10-15 01	697	2,091	0	0	0	0	362,987	362,987
10-15 02	696	2,088	0	0	0	2	361,445	380,944
10-15 03	708	2,124	0	0	0	0	367,292	367,292
10-15 04	697	2,091	0	0	0	0	362,279	362,279
10-15 05	708	2,124	0	0	0	0	367,697	367,697
10-15 06	696	2,088	0	0	0	0	361,423	361,423
10-15 07	709	2,127	0	0	0	0	374,766	577,559
10-15 08	697	2,091	0	0	0	0	364,879	410,328

The output shows how the number of executions varies over time. Figure 4.3 shows how the WISE tool allows the plotting of time-series charts for particular SQL_ID of interest:

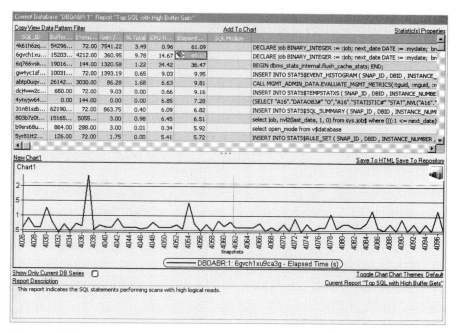

Figure 4.3: *The time-series plot for particular SQL statement.*

In the above example, the average elapsed time for the SQL statement over time is apparent. Of course, the execution speed may change due to any number of factors:

- Different bind variables

- Database resource shortage

- High physical reads from data buffer shortage

The good news is that the DBA can drill-down into those specific times when SQL statements performed badly and see exactly why execution time was slow.

The following section provides tools for identifying a CPU-constrained database.

CPU Constrained Database

The majority of wait time is spent performing computations. High wait times can also be observed when the CPU run queue exceeds the number of CPUs on the database server which can be isolated by using the "r" column in *vmstat* UNIX. Having CPU time as a top wait event is a plus for the DBA because the addition of faster CPUs or more CPUs will relieve the bottleneck.

However, high CPU usage can also be indicative of excessive Logical I/O (consistent gets) against the data buffers caused by sub-optimal SQL. It can also be indicative of shared pool and library cache contention. High CPU usage will be reported as a top timed event.

```
Top 5 Timed Events
                                                         % Total
Event                              Waits    Time (s) Ela Time
--------------------------------- ------------ ----------- --------
CPU time                           4,851       4,042     55.76
db file sequential read            1,968       1,997     27.55
log file sync                    299,097         369      5.08
db file scattered read            53,031         330      4.55
log file parallel write          302,680         190      2.62
```

The query below will extract important costing information for all objects involved in each query. SYS objects are not counted.

awr_sql_object_char.sql

```
-- ***************************************************
-- Copyright © 2005 by Rampant TechPress
-- This script is free for non-commercial purposes
-- with no warranties.  Use at your own risk.
--
-- To license this script for a commercial purpose,
-- contact info@rampant.cc
-- ***************************************************

col c1 heading 'Owner'             format a13
col c2 heading 'Object|Type'       format a15

col c3 heading 'Object|Name'       format a25
```

```
col c4 heading 'Average|CPU|Cost'    format 9,999,999
col c5 heading 'Average|IO|Cost'     format 9,999,999


break on c1 skip 2
break on c2 skip 2


select
  p.object_owner    c1,
  p.object_type     c2,
  p.object_name     c3,
  avg(p.cpu_cost)   c4,
  avg(p.io_cost)    c5
from
  dba_hist_sql_plan p
where
        p.object_name is not null
    and
        p.object_owner <> 'SYS'
group by
  p.object_owner,
  p.object_type,
  p.object_name
order by
  1,2,4 desc
;
```

The following is a sample of the output that shows the average CPU and I/O costs for all objects that participate in queries, over time periods.

Owner	Object Type	Object Name	Average CPU Cost	Average IO Cost
OLAPSYS	INDEX	CWM$CUBEDIMENSIONUSE_IDX	200	0
OLAPSYS	INDEX (UNIQUE)	CWM$DIMENSION_PK		
OLAPSYS		CWM$CUBE_PK	7,321	0
OLAPSYS		CWM$MODEL_PK	7,321	0
OLAPSYS	TABLE	CWM$CUBE	7,911	0
OLAPSYS		CWM$MODEL	7,321	0
OLAPSYS		CWM2$CUBE	7,121	2
OLAPSYS		CWM$CUBEDIMENSIONUSE	730	0
MYSCHEMA	INDEX (UNIQUE)	STATS$TIME_MODEL_STATNAME _PK	39,242	2
MYSCHEMA		CUSTOMER_DETS_PK	21,564	2
MYSCHEMA		STATS$SGASTAT_U	21,442	2
MYSCHEMA		STATS$SQL_SUMMARY_PK	16,842	2
MYSCHEMA		STATS$SQLTEXT_PK	14,442	1
MYSCHEMA		STATS$IDLE_EVENT_PK	8,171	0

```
MYSCHEMA      TABLE            CUSTOMER_DETS        5,571,375      24
MYSCHEMA                       STATS$FILE_HISTOGRAM 1,373,396       5
MYSCHEMA                       STATS$SYSTEM_EVENT     996,571       6
MYSCHEMA                       STATS$LATCH            462,161       5
MYSCHEMA                       STATS$SQL_SUMMARY      440,038       7
MYSCHEMA                       STATS$PARAMETER        361,439       5
MYSCHEMA                       STATS$FILESTATXS       224,227       3
MYSCHEMA                       STATS$WAITSTAT         144,554       3
MYSCHEMA                       STATS$TEMP_HISTOGRAM   126,304       3
MYSCHEMA                       STATS$LIBRARYCACHE     102,846       3
MYSCHEMA                       STATS$TEMPSTATXS        82,762       3
MYSCHEMA                       STATS$SGASTAT           51,807       5
MYSCHEMA                       STATS$SQLTEXT           17,781       2
MYSCHEMA                       STATS$SQL_PLAN_USAGE         0       2


SPV           INDEX (UNIQUE)   WSPV_REP_PK              7,321       0
SPV                            SPV_ALERT_DEF_PK         7,321       0


SPV           TABLE            WSPV_REPORTS           789,052      28
SPV                            SPV_MONITOR             54,092       3
SPV                            SPV_SAVED_CHARTS        38,337       3
SPV                            SPV_DB_LIST             37,487       3
SPV                            SPV_SCHED               35,607       3
SPV                            SPV_FV_STAT             35,607       3
SPV                            SPV_ALERT_DEF           15,868       1
```

The script can easily be changed to allow the entry of a table name in order to see changes in access details over time:

awr_sql_object_char_detail.sql

```
-- *************************************************
-- Copyright © 2005 by Rampant TechPress
-- This script is free for non-commercial purposes
-- with no warranties.  Use at your own risk.
--
-- To license this script for a commercial purpose,
-- contact info@rampant.cc
-- *************************************************

accept tabname prompt 'Enter Table Name:'

col c0 heading 'Begin|Interval|time'  format a8
col c1 heading 'Owner'                format a10
col c2 heading 'Object|Type'          format a10
col c3 heading 'Object|Name'          format a15
col c4 heading 'Average|CPU|Cost'     format 9,999,999
col c5 heading 'Average|IO|Cost'      format 9,999,999


break on c1 skip 2
break on c2 skip 2
```

```
select
  to_char(sn.begin_interval_time,'mm-dd hh24') c0,
  p.object_owner                               c1,
  p.object_type                                c2,
  p.object_name                                c3,
  avg(p.cpu_cost)                              c4,
  avg(p.io_cost)                               c5
from
  dba_hist_sql_plan p,
  dba_hist_sqlstat  st,
  dba_hist_snapshot sn
where
  p.object_name is not null
and
   p.object_owner <> 'SYS'
and
   p.object_name = 'CUSTOMER_DETS'
and
  p.sql_id = st.sql_id
and
  st.snap_id = sn.snap_id
group by
  to_char(sn.begin_interval_time,'mm-dd hh24'),
  p.object_owner,
  p.object_type,
  p.object_name
order by
  1,2,3 desc
;
```

This script is great because it allows the DBA to see changes to the table's access patterns over time which is a very useful feature:

Begin Interval time	Owner	Object Type	Object Name	Average CPU Cost	Average IO Cost
10-25 17	MYSCHEMA	TABLE	CUSTOMER_DETS	28,935	3
10-26 15	MYSCHEMA		CUSTOMER_DETS	28,935	3
10-27 18	MYSCHEMA		CUSTOMER_DETS	5,571,375	24
10-28 12	MYSCHEMA		CUSTOMER_DETS	28,935	3

Figure 4.4 shows how the WISE tool allows the DBA to see a time-series plot for table access pattern.

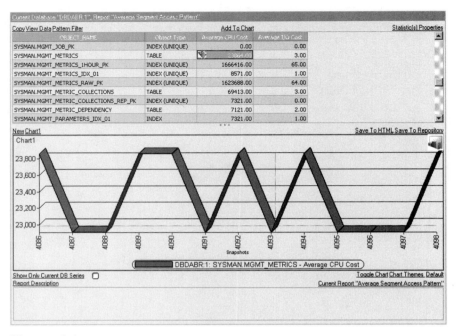

Figure 4.4: *Table access pattern plot in WISE tool.*

The next section presents tools that can be used to see when an Oracle database is RAM constrained.

RAM Constrained Database

Traditionally, the Oracle DBA measured RAM page-in operations to judge RAM utilization on the database server as shown in Figure 4.5. All Virtual Memory servers (VM) anticipate RAM shortages and asynchronously page-out RAM frames in case the RAM is required for an upcoming task.

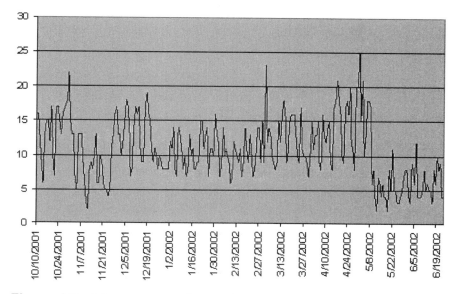

Figure 4.5: *Measurements of server RAM page-in operations.*

When the real RAM on the server is exceeded, the OS will overlay the RAM and must then page-in the saved memory frames from the swap disk on the Oracle server. However, measuring RAM usage based solely on page-ins is a mistake because the page-ins are a normal part of program start-up.

To be effective, the page-in operations must be correlated with the OS scan rate. When an Oracle server begins to run low on RAM, the page stealing daemon process awakens and UNIX begins to treat the RAM memory as a sharable resource by moving memory frames to the swap disk with paging operations.

In most UNIX and Linux implementations, the page stealing daemon operates in two modes. When the real RAM capacity is exceeded, the page stealing daemon will steal small chunks of least recently used RAM memory from a program. If RAM resource demands continue to increase beyond the real capacity of the Oracle server, the daemon escalates and begins to page-out entire programs' RAM regions.

Because of this, it is not always clear if the page-in operations are normal housekeeping or a serious memory shortage unless the activity of the page stealing daemon is correlated with the page-in output.

To aid in measuring real page-ins, the UNIX and Linux *vmstat* utility yields the scan rate (sr) column which designates the memory page scan rate. If the scan rate rises steadily, the page stealing daemon's first threshold will be identified, indicating that that particular program's entire RAM memory regions are being paged-out to the swap disk. This behavior can then be correlated with the *vmstat* page-in (pi) metric.

The following is an example from a *vmstat* output. Note the spike in the scan rate immediately preceding an increase in page-in operations.

```
oracle > vmstat 2
```

procs			memory				page				
r	b	w	avm	free	re	at	pi	po	fr	de	sr
3	0	0	144020	12778	17	9	0	14	29	0	3
3	0	0	144020	12737	15	0	1	34	4	0	8
3	0	0	144020	12360	9	0	1	46	2	0	13
1	0	0	142084	12360	5	0	3	17	0	0	21
1	0	0	142084	12360	3	0	18	0	0	0	8
1	0	0	140900	12360	1	0	34	0	0	0	0
1	0	0	140900	12360	0	0	39	0	0	0	0
1	0	0	140900	12204	0	0	3	0	0	0	0
1	0	0	137654	12204	0	0	0	0	0	0	0

The AWR has a view called *dba_hist_osstat* that stores snapshots of the *v$osstat* dynamic view; however, OS statistics indicate how the hardware and OS are working thus reflecting workload placed on the database. These statistics can give an indication of where to first search the database for possible hot spots. To view history statistics for a particular snapshot interval, use the following query:

os_stat_int_10g.sql

```
--  *************************************************
-- Copyright © 2005 by Rampant TechPress
-- This script is free for non-commercial purposes
-- with no warranties.  Use at your own risk.
--
-- To license this script for a commercial purpose,
-- contact info@rampant.cc
--  *************************************************

select e.stat_name "Statistic Name"
     , decode(e.stat_name, 'NUM_CPUS', e.value, e.value - b.value)
"Total"
     , decode( instrb(e.stat_name, 'BYTES'), 0, to_number(null)
             , round((e.value - b.value)/( select
         avg( extract( day from (e1.end_interval_time-
b1.end_interval_time) )*24*60*60+
             extract( hour from (e1.end_interval_time-
b1.end_interval_time) )*60*60+
             extract( minute from (e1.end_interval_time-
b1.end_interval_time) )*60+
             extract( second from (e1.end_interval_time-
b1.end_interval_time)) )
       from dba_hist_snapshot  b1
          ,dba_hist_snapshot  e1
      where b1.snap_id          = b.snap_id
        and e1.snap_id          = e.snap_id
        and b1.dbid             = b.dbid
        and e1.dbid             = e.dbid
        and b1.instance_number  = b.instance_number
        and e1.instance_number  = e.instance_number
        and b1.startup_time     = e1.startup_time
        and b1.end_interval_time < e1.end_interval_time ),2)) "Per
Second"
 from   dba_hist_osstat  b
      , dba_hist_osstat  e
 where b.snap_id          = &pBgnSnap
   and e.snap_id          = &pEndSnap
   and b.dbid             = &pDbId
   and e.dbid             = &pDbId
   and b.instance_number  = &pInstNum
   and e.instance_number  = &pInstNum
   and b.stat_id          = e.stat_id
   and e.value           >= b.value
   and e.value           >  0
 order by 1 asc
```

The query output looks like the following:

```
SQL> @os_stat_int_10g.sql

Statistic Name                      Total    Per Second
------------------------------  ----------   ----------
AVG_BUSY_TICKS                   1,974,925
AVG_IDLE_TICKS                   7,382,241
AVG_IN_BYTES                 2,236,256,256    23,881.91
AVG_OUT_BYTES                  566,304,768     6,047.80


AVG_SYS_TICKS                      727,533
AVG_USER_TICKS                   1,247,392
BUSY_TICKS                       1,974,925
IDLE_TICKS                       7,382,241
IN_BYTES                     2,236,256,256    23,881.91
NUM_CPUS                                 1
OUT_BYTES                      566,304,768     6,047.80
SYS_TICKS                          727,533
USER_TICKS                        1247,392
```

The *os_stat_int_10g.sql* script allows a view of OS statistics in two forms: cumulative and per second. With this information, it is easy to identify and correct *hot* areas in the OS and hardware.

The WISE tool has a corresponding report called OS Statistics that is used to produce history charts for operating system metrics. This sophisticated display has virtually every Oracle internal and OS metric, all in a single display, making it easier to find external bottlenecks. Figure 4.6 shows a sample of the WISE chart.

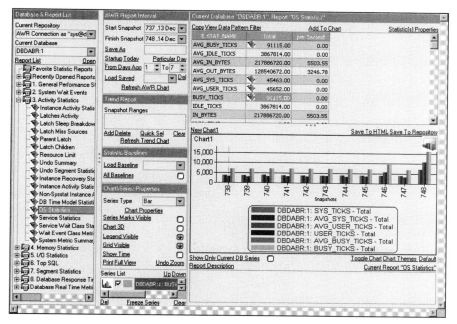

Figure 4.6: *AWR OS Statistics chart in WISE.*

The next section will examine how to find out if an Oracle database has network constraint issues.

Network Constrained Database

Network bottlenecks are common in distributed systems and those with high network traffic. Such bottlenecks manifest as SQL*Net wait events as evidenced by the AWR Report:

```
Top 5 Wait Events

                                                      % Total
Event                            Waits      Time (cs) Wt Time
-------------------------------- ----------- --------- -------
SQL*Net more data to client      3,914,935  9,475,372   99.76
db file sequential read          1,367,659      6,129     .06
db file parallel write               7,582      5,001     .05
rdbms ipc reply                         26      4,612     .05
db file scattered read              16,886      2,446     .03
```

Server stats can be viewed in a variety of ways using standard server tools such as *vmstat, glance, top* and *sar.* The goal is to ensure that the database server has enough CPU and RAM resources at all times in order to manage the Oracle requests.

Server stress can change radically over time. The system might be CPU-bound in the morning and network-bound in the afternoon. The challenge is to identify server stress over time and learn to interpret any trends in hardware consumption. For example, Oracle10g Enterprise Manager tracks server run queue waits over time and combines the CPU and Paging display into a single EM screen so that DBAs can tell when the system is experiencing server-side waits on hardware resources. A sample of the display is shown in Figure 4.7.

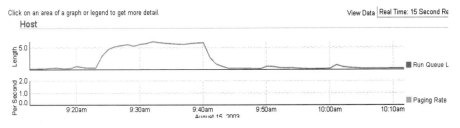

Figure 4.7: *OEM Server run queue and RAM paging values.*

This time based display is important because it illustrates how Oracle performance issues can be transient with short spikes of excessive hardware consumption. Considering the super-fast nature of CPU dispatching, a database might be CPU constrained for a few minutes at a time several times per day. The time series EM display gives a quick visual clue about those times when the system is experiencing a CPU or RAM bottleneck.

The next step in the process involves drilling down to look at the overall tuning of the Oracle instance.

Proactive Oracle Instance Tuning

As a quick review, an Oracle instance is the allocated RAM region on the server, which is called the System Global Area (SGA), and a set of running programs that do the work for the instance, which are called background processes.

Instance tuning will be discussed in great detail in the chapter on Oracle silver bullet parameters, but this section will provide a quick overview.

Oracle instance tuning consists of the adjustment of the static global parameters that affect Oracle performance. The process begins with an examination of the instance to locate bottlenecks.

There is a standard AWR report which contains a Wait Events section that displays top wait events. The following query can also be used to allow retrieval of top wait events for a particular AWR snapshot interval:

wt_events_int_10g.sql

```
-- *************************************************
-- Copyright © 2005 by Rampant TechPress
-- This script is free for non-commercial purposes
-- with no warranties.  Use at your own risk.
--
-- To license this script for a commercial purpose,
-- contact info@rampant.cc
-- *************************************************

select event
     , waits "Waits"
     , time "Wait Time (s)"
     , pct*100 "Percent of Total"
     , waitclass "Wait Class"
from (select e.event_name event
                    , e.total_waits - nvl(b.total_waits,0)  waits
                    , (e.time_waited_micro - nvl(b.time_waited_micro,0))/1000000  time
                    , (e.time_waited_micro - nvl(b.time_waited_micro,0))/
                      (select sum(e1.time_waited_micro - nvl(b1.time_waited_micro,0)) from
dba_hist_system_event b1 , dba_hist_system_event e1
                    where b1.snap_id(+)            = b.snap_id
                      and e1.snap_id               = e.snap_id
                      and b1.dbid(+)               = b.dbid
                      and e1.dbid                  = e.dbid
                      and b1.instance_number(+)    = b.instance_number
                      and e1.instance_number       = e.instance_number
                      and b1.event_id(+)           = e1.event_id
```

```
                  and el.total_waits              > nvl(bl.total_waits,0)
                  and el.wait_class               <> 'Idle'
    ) pct
                      , e.wait_class waitclass
             from
                 dba_hist_system_event b ,
                 dba_hist_system_event e
             where b.snap_id(+)                 = &pBgnSnap
                and e.snap_id                   = &pEndSnap
                and b.dbid(+)                   = &pDbId
                and e.dbid                      = &pDbId
                and b.instance_number(+)        = &pInstNum
                and e.instance_number           = &pInstNum
                and b.event_id(+)               = e.event_id
                and e.total_waits               > nvl(b.total_waits,0)
                and e.wait_class                <> 'Idle'
        order by time desc, waits desc
        )
```

The sample output of this query looks like:

```
SQL> @ wt_events_int_10g.sql

EVENT                          Waits Wait Time (s) Percent of Total Wait Class
------------------------------ ----- ------------- ---------------- -------------
control file parallel write    11719        119.13 34,1611762       System I/O
class slave wait                  20        102.46 29,3801623       Other
Queue Monitor Task Wait           74         66.74 19,1371008       Other
log file sync                    733         20.60 5,90795938       Commit
db file sequential read         1403         14.27 4,09060416       User I/O
log buffer space                 178         10.17 2,91745801       Configuration
process startup                  114          7.65 2,19243344       Other
db file scattered read           311          2.14 ,612767501       User I/O
control file sequential read    7906          1.33 ,380047642       System I/O
latch free                       254          1.13 ,324271668       Other
log file switch completion        20          1.11 ,319292495       Configuration
```

The output of the *wt_events_int_10g.sql* script displays the wait events ordered by wait times in seconds. The WISE tool has a report named "Top Wait Events" that yields a chart for top wait events that occurred for the particular snapshot interval as shown in Figure 4.8.

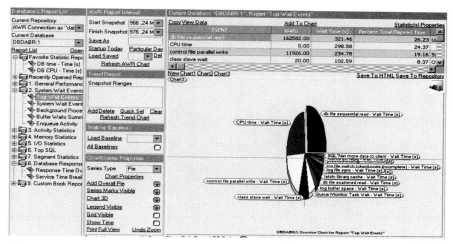

Figure 4.8: *AWR Top Wait Events chart in WISE.*

The following query can be used to retrieve background wait event data for a particular snapshot interval:

bg_event_int_10g.sql

```
--  *************************************************
--  Copyright © 2005 by Rampant TechPress
--  This script is free for non-commercial purposes
--  with no warranties.  Use at your own risk.
--
--  To license this script for a commercial purpose,
--  contact info@rampant.cc
--  *************************************************

select
      event "Event Name",
      waits "Waits",
      timeouts "Timeouts",
      time "Wait Time (s)",
      avgwait "Avg Wait (ms)",
      waitclass "Wait Class"
from
      (select e.event_name event
            , e.total_waits - nvl(b.total_waits,0)  waits
            , e.total_timeouts - nvl(b.total_timeouts,0) timeouts
            , (e.time_waited_micro -
nvl(b.time_waited_micro,0))/1000000  time
            , decode ((e.total_waits - nvl(b.total_waits, 0)), 0,
to_number(NULL),
```

```
          ((e.time_waited_micro -
nvl(b.time_waited_micro,0))/1000) / (e.total_waits -
nvl(b.total_waits,0)) ) avgwait
         , e.wait_class waitclass
    from
       dba_hist_bg_event_summary b ,
       dba_hist_bg_event_summary e
    where
                 b.snap_id(+)            = &pBgnSnap
             and e.snap_id               = &pEndSnap
             and b.dbid(+)               = &pDbId
             and e.dbid                  = &pDbId
             and b.instance_number(+)    = &pInstNum
             and e.instance_number       = &pInstNum
             and b.event_id(+)           = e.event_id
             and e.total_waits           > nvl(b.total_waits,0)
             and e.wait_class            <> 'Idle' )
order by time desc, waits desc
```

The WISE tool has a corresponding report named "Background Process Wait Events" that allows users to build time-series charts for background wait events as shown in Figure 4.9.

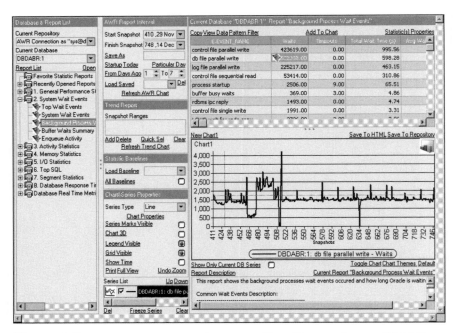

Figure 4.9: *AWR Background Process Wait Events chart in WISE.*

The output of *bg_event_int_10g.sql* script looks similar to the output of *sys_event_int_10g.sql* with the exception that wait events are displayed for background processes.

The next section provides information on Oracle object silver bullets.

Oracle Object Tuning

Oracle object tuning is the process of setting characteristics for data files, tablespaces, tables, indexes and IOTs with the goal of achieving optimal performance. Each new release of Oracle introduces new object-level parameters for DBAs to use:

- **Oracle 7** - Bitmap Indexes

- **Oracle8** - Locally Managed Tablespaces (LMTs)

- **Oracle9i** - Automatic Segment Space Management (ASSM)

- **Oracle10g** - Automatic Storage Management (ASM)

Object tuning can be vital to overall system performance because major system wait events, such as buffer busy waits, are closely tied to the internal structure of the database objects. For example, the following adjustments might be called for:

- **Tablespaces** - There are many tablespace options including dictionary managed tablespaces, Locally Managed Tablespaces, and special tablespace options such as Automatic Segment Space (ASS) managed tablespaces (bitmap freelists).

- **Indexes** - Users can now choose between b*tree, bitmap and star indexes.

- **Tables/Indexes** - Users can adjust the number of freelists, freelist groups and the freelist un-link threshold (PCTFREE) at the object level.

The following script, *wait_time_detail.sql*, compares the wait event values from *dba_hist_waitstat* and *dba_hist_active_sess_history*. This allows the identification of the exact objects that are experiencing wait events.

wait_time_detail.sql

```
-- *****************************************************
-- Copyright © 2005 by Rampant TechPress
-- This script is free for non-commercial purposes
-- with no warranties.  Use at your own risk.
--
-- To license this script for a commercial purpose,
-- contact info@rampant.cc
-- *****************************************************

set pages 999
set lines 80

break on snap_time skip 2

col snap_time      heading 'Snap|Time'    format a20
col file_name      heading 'File|Name'    format a40
col object_type    heading 'Object|Type'  format a10
col object_name    heading 'Object|Name'  format a20
col wait_count     heading 'Wait|Count'   format 999,999
col time           heading 'Time'         format 999,999

select
   to_char(begin_interval_time,'yyyy-mm-dd hh24:mi') snap_time,
--    file_name,
   object_type,
   object_name,
   wait_count,
   time
from
   dba_hist_waitstat              wait,
   dba_hist_snapshot              snap,
   dba_hist_active_sess_history   ash,
   dba_data_files                 df,
   dba_objects                    obj
where
   wait.snap_id = snap.snap_id
and
   wait.snap_id = ash.snap_id
and
```

```
    df.file_id = ash.current_file#
and
    obj.object_id = ash.current_obj#
and
    wait_count > 50
order by
    to_char(begin_interval_time,'yyyy-mm-dd hh24:mi'),
    file_name
;
```

This script is enabled to join into the *dba_data_files* view to get the file names associated with the wait event. This is a very powerful script that can be used to quickly drill-in to find the cause of specific waits. The following is a sample output:

```
SQL> @wait_time_detail


This will compare values from dba_hist_waitstat with
detail information from dba_hist_active_sess_history.
```

Snap Time	Object Type	Object Name	Wait Count	Time
2004-02-28 01:00	TABLE	ORDOR	4,273	67
	INDEX	PK_CUST_ID	12,373	324
	INDEX	FK_CUST_NAME	3,883	17
2004-02-29 03:00	TABLE	ITEM_DETAIL	83	69
2004-03-01 04:00	TABLE	ITEM_DETAIL	1,246	45
2004-03-01 21:00	TABLE	CUSTOMER_DET	4,381	354
	TABLE	IND_PART	117	15
2004-03-04 01:00	TABLE	MARVIN	41,273	16
	TABLE	FACTOTUM	2,827	43
	TABLE	DOW_KNOB	853	6
	TABLE	ITEM_DETAIL	57	331
	TABLE	HIST_ORD	4,337	176

Adjusting the structure of Oracle objects can help remove system bottlenecks. The value of removing these bottlenecks will be presented in Chapter 7, *Instance Parameter Silver Bullets.*

The next section provides information on Oracle SQL tuning silver bullets.

Oracle SQL Tuning

SQL tuning is a complex subject and entire books have been dedicated to the endeavor. In essence, SQL tuning activities have the following goals:

- **Eliminate Sub-Optimal Large-Table Full-Table Scans** – This ensures that the fastest access path to the data is chosen.

- **Ensure Fastest Table Join Method** - The optimizer chooses intelligently between nested loop joins, hash joins and star join methods.

- **Ensure Optimal Table-Joining Order** - SQL will run fastest when the first table joins deliver the smallest result set.

In Oracle10g, the new SQL profiles and the SQL Access advisor can be used to help identify sub-optimal SQL statements. Once identified, the new Oracle10g SQL profile utility will allow changes to execution plans without adding hints. Holistic SQL tuning will be covered in greater detail in a later chapter.

The following is an amazing script that will show the access patterns of usage over time. If a DBA really wants to know their system, understanding how SQL accesses the tables and indexes in their database can provide them with amazing insights.

The optimal instance configuration for large-table full-table scans is quite different than the configuration for an OLTP database. This handy report will quickly identify changes in table access patterns.

💾 awr_sql_scan_sums.sql

```
-- *************************************************
-- Copyright © 2005 by Rampant TechPress
-- This script is free for non-commercial purposes
-- with no warranties.  Use at your own risk.
--
-- To license this script for a commercial purpose,
-- contact info@rampant.cc
-- *************************************************

col c1  heading 'Begin|Interval|Time'            format a20
col c2  heading 'Large|Table|Full Table|Scans'   format 999,999
col c3  heading 'Small|Table|Full Table|Scans'   format 999,999
col c4  heading 'Total|Index|Scans'              format 999,999


select
  f.c1  c1,
  f.c2  c2,
  s.c2  c3,
  i.c2  c4
from
(
select
  to_char(sn.begin_interval_time,'yy-mm-dd hh24')  c1,
  count(1)                          c2
from
  dba_hist_sql_plan p,
  dba_hist_sqlstat  s,
  dba_hist_snapshot sn,
  dba_segments      o
where
  p.object_owner <> 'SYS'
and
  p.object_owner = o.owner
and
  p.object_name = o.segment_name
and
  o.blocks > 1000
and
  p.operation like '%TABLE ACCESS%'
and
  p.options like '%FULL%'
and
  p.sql_id = s.sql_id
and
  s.snap_id = sn.snap_id
group by
  to_char(sn.begin_interval_time,'yy-mm-dd hh24')
order by
1 ) f,
(
select
  to_char(sn.begin_interval_time,'yy-mm-dd hh24')  c1,
```

```
   count(1)                                    c2
from
   dba_hist_sql_plan  p,
   dba_hist_sqlstat   s,
   dba_hist_snapshot  sn,
   dba_segments       o
where
   p.object_owner <> 'SYS'
and
   p.object_owner = o.owner
and
   p.object_name = o.segment_name
and
   o.blocks < 1000
and
   p.operation like '%INDEX%'
and
   p.sql_id = s.sql_id
and
   s.snap_id = sn.snap_id
group by
   to_char(sn.begin_interval_time,'yy-mm-dd hh24')
order by
1 ) s,
(
select
   to_char(sn.begin_interval_time,'yy-mm-dd hh24')  c1,
   count(1)                                    c2
from
   dba_hist_sql_plan  p,
   dba_hist_sqlstat   s,
   dba_hist_snapshot  sn
where
   p.object_owner <> 'SYS'
and
   p.operation like '%INDEX%'
and
   p.sql_id = s.sql_id
and
   s.snap_id = sn.snap_id
group by
   to_char(sn.begin_interval_time,'yy-mm-dd hh24')
order by
1 ) i
where
      f.c1 = s.c1
   and
      f.c1 = i.c1
;
```

The sample output is shown below and contains a comparison of
index vs. table scan access. This is a very important signature for

---

any database because it indicates, at a glance, the balance between index (OLTP) and data warehouse type access.

Begin Interval Time	Full	Large Table Table Scans	Full	Small Table Table Scans	Total Index Scans
04-10-22 15		2		19	21
04-10-22 16				1	1
04-10-25 10				18	20
04-10-25 17		9		15	17
04-10-25 18		1		19	22
04-10-25 21				19	24
04-10-26 12				23	28
04-10-26 13		3		17	19
04-10-26 14				18	19
04-10-26 15		11		4	7
04-10-26 16		4		18	18
04-10-26 17				17	19
04-10-26 18		3		17	17
04-10-27 13		2		17	19
04-10-27 14		3		17	19
04-10-27 15		4		17	18
04-10-27 16				17	17
04-10-27 17		3		17	20
04-10-27 18		17		20	22
04-10-27 19		1		20	26
04-10-28 12		22		17	20
04-10-28 13		2		17	17
04-10-29 13		9		18	19

This is an important report because it shows how Oracle is accessing data over time periods. This is especially important because it shows when the database processing modality shifts between OLTP (*first_rows* index access) to a batch reporting mode (*all_rows* full scans) as shown in Figure 4.10.

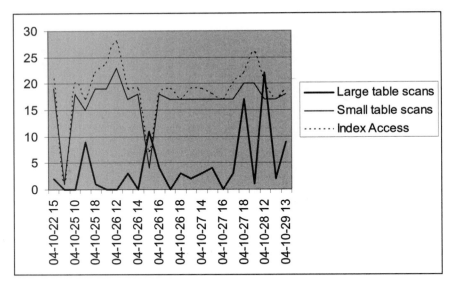

Figure 4.10: *Plot of full scans vs. index access.*

The example in Figure 4.10 is typical of an OLTP database with the majority of access being via small-table full-table scans and index access. In this case, the DBA needs to carefully check the large-table full-table scans, verify their legitimacy (i.e. no missing indexes), and adjust them to maximize their throughput.

In a really busy database, there may be concurrent OLTP index access and full-table scans for reports. It is the DBA's job to know the specific times when the database shifts table access modes as well as those tables that experience the changes.

Conclusion

This chapter has provided an overview of the proactive holistic approach to Oracle tuning. The main points of this chapter include:

- It is very difficult to tune Oracle when an external anomaly is hindering performance. Always verify the server environment first by checking CPU, RAM Network and disk, especially RAID. All tuning activities start with a global review of the server (e.g. CPU, network, disk) to isolate the current hardware bottleneck.

- Reactive tuning is too little, too late. The end-user is already experiencing a loss of service.

- Proactive tuning assumes that DBAs take advantage of the Oracle dynamic tuning features and change the system configuration just-in-time to meet the change in processing demand.

- Before tuning individual SQL statements make sure that the instance is properly optimized for the current workload. In Oracle10g, AMM should be used or dynamic SGA features employed to ensure that the SGA remains optimized when processing patterns change.

The next chapter provides a more detailed examination of the concept of Silver Bullets and how holistic changes can improve Oracle performance.

Very Large Database Silver Bullets

"I can remove evil spirits from your data warehouse"

Tuning in Terabytes

As corporate data warehouse systems grow from small-scale applications into industry-wide systems, the IT manager must maintain a posture of growth without service interruption. Oracle10g fills this niche with a database that allows infinite scalability; however, the IT manager must also choose server hardware that allows seamless growth.

Since the earliest days of Decision Support Systems (DSS) of the 1960s, database professionals have recognized that internal processing for data warehouse applications is very different from Online Transaction Processing systems (OLTP). Data warehouse applications tend to be very I/O intensive, as the database reads trillions of bytes of information. Data warehouse systems require specialized servers that can support the typical processing that exist in data warehouses.

Most data warehouses are bi-modal and have batch windows, usually in the evenings, when new data is loaded, indexed, and summarized. The server must have on demand CPU and RAM resources, and the database management system must be able to dynamically reconfigure its resources to accommodate these shifts in processing.

Oracle Parallel Query

To process large volumes of data quickly, the server must be able to support parallel, large-table-full-table scans for data warehouse aggregation. One of the most significant improvements in multi-CPU servers is their ability to utilize Oracle parallel features for table summarization, aggregation, DBA maintenance (table reorganization), and parallel data manipulation.

For example, this divide-and-conquer approach makes large-table-full-table scans run seven times faster on an eight-CPU server and 15 times faster on a 16-way SMP server. Figure 5.1 is a graphical representation of this process.

- **Full-table scans can run 15x faster**
- **Parallel DML**
- **Parallel table reorganizations**

Figure 5.1: *Data warehouse large-table-full-table scans.*

Historically, data warehouse applications have been constrained by I/O, but this is changing with the introduction of specialized data warehouse techniques while maintaining the goal of keeping the server CPUs running at full capacity.

Large RAM Regions

Oracle10g also offers Automatic Memory Management (AMM). With this feature, Oracle10g will automatically reassign RAM frames between the *db_cache_size* and the *pga_aggregate_target* region to maximize throughput of the data warehouse.

The advent of large RAM regions is also beneficial for the data warehouse. In most data warehouses, a giant, central fact table exists. This central fact table is surrounded by smaller dimension tables as shown in Figure 5.2.

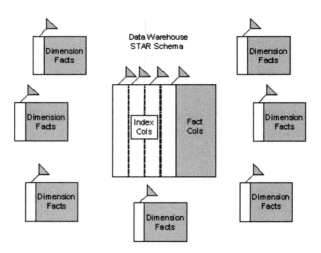

Figure 5.2: *A typical data warehouse schema.*

In a typical STAR schema, the super-large full-table scans can never be cached, but it is important to be able to control the caching of the dimension tables and indexes. When using a 64-bit server with fast RAM access, the Oracle KEEP pool and multiple buffer caches can be configured to guarantee that the smaller, frequently referenced objects always remain in the data buffers. This shifts the database bottleneck away from I/O. Once the bottleneck has shifted from I/O to CPU, the DBA is in a position to scale performance by adding additional processors.

The large data buffer caches in most OLTP Oracle systems make them CPU-bound, but Oracle data warehouses are another story. With terabytes of information to aggregate and summarize, most Oracle data warehouses are I/O-bound, and the DBA must choose a server that optimizes disk I/O throughput.

Oracle has always made very large database (VLDB) technology a priority as evidenced by their introduction of partitioned structures, advanced bitmap indexing, and materialized views. Oracle10g provides some features that are ideal for the data warehouse application.

It is not difficult to determine when an Oracle warehouse is disk I/O bound. In the following AWR report (STATSPACK report for Oracle9i and earlier), a typical data warehouse system is shown that is clearly constrained by disk I/O. This constraint results from the high percentage of full-object scans and multi-block reads.

```
Top 5 Timed Events
~~~~~~~~~~~~~~~~~~
                                                        % Total
Event                     Waits           Time (s)     Ela Time
------------------------- --------------- ------------- --------
db file scattered read            2,598         7,146      58.54
db file sequential read          25,519         3,246      12.04
library cache load lock             673         1,363       9.26
CPU time                                        1,154       7.83
log file parallel write          19,157           837       5.68
```

It is apparent from the results that scattered reads, full-table scans, constitute the majority of the total database time. This is very typical of a data warehouse that performs aggregations via SQL. This is also common during the refresh period for Oracle materialized views. The problem is the I/O bottleneck that is introduced during these periods.

Since the typical data warehouse is data intensive, there is always a problem fully utilizing the CPU power. UNISYS has addressed this issue by leveraging Non-Uniform Memory Access (NUMA), whereby Windows and Oracle10g are automatically configured to exploit NUMA to keep the CPUs busy. The data buffer hit ratio is not relevant for data warehouses or for systems that commonly perform full-table scans or those that use *all_rows* SQL optimization.

While a 30 GB *db_cache_size* might be appropriate for an OLTP shop or a shop that uses a large working set, a super-large SGA does not benefit data warehouses and decision support systems in which most data access is performed by a parallelized full-table scan. When Oracle performs a parallel full-table scan, the database blocks are read directly into the Program Global Area (PGA), bypassing the data buffer RAM. Figure 5.3 shows this process.

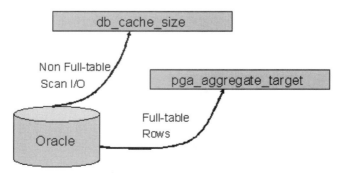

Figure 5.3: *Parallel Full Scans Bypass SGA data buffers.*

In the figure above, having a large *db_cache_size* does not benefit parallel large-table-full-table scans, as this requires memory in the *pga_aggregate_target* region instead. With Oracle 10g, the multiple data buffer features can be used to segregate and cache the dimension tables and indexes, all while providing sufficient RAM for the full scans. When the processing mode changes for evening ETL and rollups, Oracle10g AMM will automatically detect the change in data access and re-allocate the RAM regions to accommodate the current processing.

Oracle data warehouses are very different in their processing requirements, but there are some general silver bullets such as materialized views that are extremely important for all very large Oracle databases.

Oracle Materialized Views

In the world of database architecture, the need to dynamically create complex objects conflicts with the demand for sub-second response time. Oracle's answer to this dilemma is the materialized view. Database designers can use materialized views to pre-join tables, presort solution sets, and pre-summarize complex data warehouse information.

Since this work is completed in advance, it gives end users the illusion of instantaneous response time. Materialized views are especially useful for Oracle data warehouses, where cross-tabulations often take hours to perform. The Oracle DBA must understand the internals of materialized views and demonstrate how to pre-compute complex aggregates, having Oracle dynamically rewrite SQL to reference pre-computed aggregate information.

Materialized views are a true silver bullet that allows the repair of bad schema normalization by pre-joining tables and pre-summarizing data values. Best of all, Oracle materialized views are integrated with the Oracle 10g query re-write facility. This means that any queries that might benefit from the pre-summarization will be automatically rewritten to reference the aggregate view, thereby avoiding a very expensive and unnecessary large-table-full-table scan.

The Oracle10g *dbms_advisor* utility will automatically detect and recommend materialized view definitions. This utility will then create a materialized view to reduce disk I/O, as will the Oracle10g SQL Tuning Advisor.

In terms of aggregation, materialized views improve query speed by rewriting a query against the base table with a query against the pre-aggregated summary table via the following:

- **Pre-calculated Summaries** - The s*um, avg, min, max, count(*), count(distinct x)* functions are utilized.

- **Pre-joined Tables** - Tables are pre-joined to improve performance.

Materialized views are especially useful for Oracle data warehouses, where cross-tabulations often take hours to perform.

Materialized Views and Snapshots

Materialized views are an introduction of redundancy, along the same lines as Oracle snapshots. When an Oracle materialized view is created, Oracle treats the materialized view just as it would an Oracle snapshot. Oracle requires the specification of a schedule for periodic updates.

Updates are accomplished by way of a refresh interval, which can range from instantaneous rebuilding of the materialized view to a hot refresh that occurs weekly.

Prior to Oracle8, DBA's using summaries spent a significant amount of time manually identifying which views to create. The DBA must then create, index, and update them as well as advising their users which ones to use. Manual Oracle Aggregation is shown in Figure 5.4.

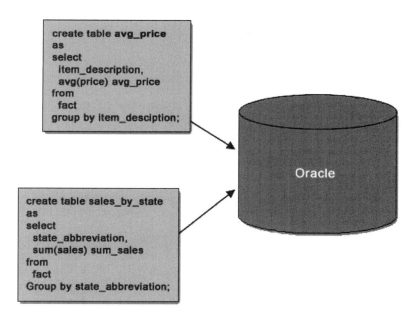

Figure 5.4: *Manual Oracle Aggregation.*

The problem with manually creating summary tables is that the DBA has to direct the end user to the new table. There was no Oracle mechanism to automatically rewrite the SQL to go to the pre-created summary. Materialized views provide an alternate approach.

Automatic SQL Query Re-write

The query optimizer automatically recognizes when an existing materialized view can be used to satisfy a request. It transparently rewrites the request to use the materialized view. Queries are then directed to the materialized view and not to the underlying detail tables, resulting in a significant performance gain.

The Oracle SQL optimizer now has other query rewrite capabilities. It often rewrites correlated subqueries into standard joins. For example, starting in Oracle9i the SQL optimizer automatically detects situations in which someone uses a *not exists* clause with an uncorrelated subquery and replaces the SQL with an equivalent query that runs much faster using a standard order outer join with a not null criterion.

The following is the SQL query before rewrite:

```
select
   customer_name from customer
where
   not exists (select customer_name from bad_credit);
```

This is the same query after automatic query rewrite:

```
select customer_name
from customer c, bad_credit b
where b.customer_name(+) = c.customer_name
and b.customer_name is null;
```

Oracle is very sophisticated in its SQL query rewrite capability. The Oracle DBA can control the propensity of the SQL optimizer to go to the materialized views to service the query. The options are as follows:

- **Full SQL Text Match** - In this method, the SQL text of the query's *select statement* clause is compared to the SQL text of the *select* clause in the materialized view's defining query.

- **Partial Text Match** - If a full SQL test match fails, the optimizer will attempt a partial SQL text match. The optimizer compares the remaining SQL text of the query, beginning with the *from* clause, to the remaining SQL text of the materialized view's defining query.

- **No Match** - If the full and partial SQL text matches both fail, the optimizer uses general query rewrite methods that enable the use of a materialized view even if it contains only part of the data or data that can be converted.

When using query rewrite, materialized views satisfying the largest number of SQL queries are created. For example, if 20 queries commonly applied to the detail or fact tables are identified, it may be possible to satisfy them with five or six well-written materialized views.

The *dbms_mview* package and the Oracle10g SQL Tuning advisor now makes recommendations for intelligent Materialized View creation.

In sum, Oracle's introduction of materialized views significantly improves the performance of Oracle systems required to process complex SQL statements while delivering sub-second response time.

Use Materialized Views

There was a point-of-sale data warehouse that was used for ad-hoc queries by end users in the Marketing department.

It became immediately apparent that a new end user was performing ad-hoc queries and that nearly every query in the library cache was performing a *sum()* or *avg()* function against several key tables.

The *v$sql_plan* view via *plan9i.sql* or *plan10g.sql* showed a considerable number of very-large-table full-table scans, and the system was virtually crippled by "db file scattered read" waits as shown here in an AWR report.

```
Top 5 Timed Events
                                                  % Total
Event                        Waits   Time (s) Ela Time
---------------------------  -------  --------  --------
db file scattered read       325,519    3,246    82.04
library cache load lock        4,673    1,363     9.26
db file sequential read      534,598    7,146     4.54
CPU time                       1,154      645     3.83
log file parallel write       19,157      837     1.68
```

The *plan9i.sql* and *plan10.sql* scripts are listed below. They will be referenced in later sections of this book and are also available in the on-line Code Depot.

🖫 **plan9i.sql**

```
-- with no warranties.  Use at your own risk.
--
-- To license this script for a commercial purpose,
-- contact info@rampant.cc
-- ************************************************

set echo off;
set feedback on

set pages 999;
column nbr_FTS   format 999,999
column num_rows  format 999,999,999
column blocks    format 999,999
column owner     format a14;
column name      format a24;
column ch        format a1;

column object_owner heading "Owner"              format a12;
column ct               heading "# of SQL selects" format 999,999;

select
   object_owner,
   count(*)    ct
from
   v$sql_plan
where
   object_owner is not null
group by
   object_owner
order by
   ct desc
;
--spool access.lst;

set heading off;
set feedback off;

set heading on;
set feedback on;
ttitle 'full table scans and counts|  |The "K" indicates that the
table is in the KEEP Pool (Oracle8).'
select
   p.owner,
   p.name,
   t.num_rows,
--    ltrim(t.cache) ch,
   decode(t.buffer_pool,'KEEP','Y','DEFAULT','N') K,
   s.blocks blocks,
   sum(a.executions) nbr_FTS
from
   dba_tables    t,
   dba_segments s,
   v$sqlarea      a,
   (select distinct
     address,
     object_owner owner,
     object_name name
```

```
   from
      v$sql_plan
   where
      operation = 'TABLE ACCESS'
      and
      options = 'FULL') p
where
   a.address = p.address
   and
   t.owner = s.owner
   and
   t.table_name = s.segment_name
   and
   t.table_name = p.name
   and
   t.owner = p.owner
   and
   t.owner not in ('SYS','SYSTEM')
having
   sum(a.executions) > 9
group by
   p.owner, p.name, t.num_rows, t.cache, t.buffer_pool, s.blocks
order by
   sum(a.executions) desc;

column nbr_RID  format 999,999,999
column num_rows format 999,999,999
column owner    format a15;
column name     format a25;

ttitle 'Table access by ROWID and counts'
select
   p.owner,
   p.name,
   t.num_rows,
   sum(s.executions) nbr_RID
from
   dba_tables t,
   v$sqlarea s,
   (select distinct
      address,
      object_owner owner,
      object_name name
   from
      v$sql_plan
   where
      operation = 'TABLE ACCESS'
      and
      options = 'BY ROWID') p
where
   s.address = p.address
   and
   t.table_name = p.name
   and
   t.owner = p.owner
having
   sum(s.executions) > 9
```

```
group by
   p.owner, p.name, t.num_rows
order by
   sum(s.executions) desc;

--***************************************************
--  Index Report Section
--***************************************************

column nbr_scans  format 999,999,999
column num_rows   format 999,999,999
column tbl_blocks format 999,999,999
column owner      format a9;
column table_name format a20;
column index_name format a20;

ttitle 'Index full scans and counts'
select
   p.owner,
   d.table_name,
   p.name index_name,
   seg.blocks tbl_blocks,
   sum(s.executions) nbr_scans
from
   dba_segments seg,
   v$sqlarea s,
   dba_indexes d,
   (select distinct
      address,
      object_owner owner,
      object_name name
   from
      v$sql_plan
   where
      operation = 'INDEX'
      and
      options = 'FULL SCAN') p
where
   d.index_name = p.name
   and
   s.address = p.address
   and
   d.table_name = seg.segment_name
   and
   seg.owner = p.owner
having
   sum(s.executions) > 9
group by
   p.owner, d.table_name, p.name, seg.blocks
order by
   sum(s.executions) desc;

ttitle 'Index range scans and counts'
select
   p.owner,
   d.table_name,
   p.name index_name,
```

```
      seg.blocks tbl_blocks,
   sum(s.executions) nbr_scans
from
   dba_segments seg,
   v$sqlarea s,
   dba_indexes d,
   (select distinct
      address,
      object_owner owner,
      object_name name
    from
       v$sql_plan

    where
       operation = 'INDEX'
       and
       options = 'RANGE SCAN') p
where
   d.index_name = p.name
   and
   s.address = p.address
   and
   d.table_name = seg.segment_name
   and
   seg.owner = p.owner
having
   sum(s.executions) > 9
group by
   p.owner, d.table_name, p.name, seg.blocks
order by
   sum(s.executions) desc;

ttitle 'Index unique scans and counts'
select
   p.owner,
   d.table_name,
   p.name index_name,
   sum(s.executions) nbr_scans
from
   v$sqlarea s,
   dba_indexes d,
   (select distinct
      address,
      object_owner owner,
      object_name name
    from
       v$sql_plan
    where
       operation = 'INDEX'
       and
       options = 'UNIQUE SCAN') p
where
   d.index_name = p.name
   and
   s.address = p.address
having
   sum(s.executions) > 9
```

```
group by
   p.owner, d.table_name, p.name
order by
   sum(s.executions) desc;
```

plan10g.sql

```
-- ****************************************************
-- Copyright © 2005 by Rampant TechPress
-- This script is free for non-commercial purposes
-- with no warranties.  Use at your own risk.
--
-- To license this script for a commercial purpose,
-- contact info@rampant.cc
-- ****************************************************

spool plan.lst

set echo off
set feedback on

set pages 999;
column nbr_FTS  format 99,999
column num_rows format 999,999
column blocks   format 9,999
column owner    format a10;
column name     format a30;
column ch       format a1;
column time        heading "Snapshot Time"          format a15

column object_owner heading "Owner"               format a12;
column ct           heading "# of SQL selects" format 999,999;

break on time

select
   object_owner,
   count(*)    ct
from
   dba_hist_sql_plan
where
   object_owner is not null
group by
   object_owner
order by
   ct desc
;

--spool access.lst;

set heading on;
set feedback on;
```

```
ttitle 'full table scans and counts|    |The "K" indicates that the
table is in the KEEP Pool (Oracle8).'
select
   to_char(sn.end_interval_time,'mm/dd/rr hh24') time,
   p.owner,
   p.name,
   t.num_rows,
--    ltrim(t.cache) ch,
   decode(t.buffer_pool,'KEEP','Y','DEFAULT','N') K,
   s.blocks blocks,
   sum(a.executions_delta) nbr_FTS
from
   dba_tables     t,
   dba_segments s,
   dba_hist_sqlstat      a,
   dba_hist_snapshot sn,
   (select distinct
     pl.sql_id,
     object_owner owner,
     object_name name
   from
     dba_hist_sql_plan pl
   where
     operation = 'TABLE ACCESS'
     and
     options = 'FULL') p
where
   a.snap_id = sn.snap_id
   and
   a.sql_id = p.sql_id
   and
   t.owner = s.owner
   and
   t.table_name = s.segment_name
   and
   t.table_name = p.name
   and
   t.owner = p.owner
   and
   t.owner not in ('SYS','SYSTEM')
having
   sum(a.executions_delta) > 1
group by
   to_char(sn.end_interval_time,'mm/dd/rr hh24'),p.owner, p.name,
t.num_rows, t.cache, t.buffer_pool, s.blocks
order by
   1 asc;

column nbr_RID  format 999,999,999
column num_rows format 999,999,999
column owner    format a15;
column name     format a25;

ttitle 'Table access by ROWID and counts'
select
   to_char(sn.end_interval_time,'mm/dd/rr hh24') time,
   p.owner,
```

```
      p.name,
      t.num_rows,
      sum(a.executions_delta) nbr_RID
from
      dba_tables t,
      dba_hist_sqlstat     a,
      dba_hist_snapshot sn,
     (select distinct
        pl.sql_id,
        object_owner owner,
        object_name name
      from
        dba_hist_sql_plan pl
      where
        operation = 'TABLE ACCESS'
        and
        options = 'BY USER ROWID') p
where
      a.snap_id = sn.snap_id
      and
      a.sql_id = p.sql_id
      and
      t.table_name = p.name
      and
      t.owner = p.owner
having
      sum(a.executions_delta) > 9
group by
      to_char(sn.end_interval_time,'mm/dd/rr hh24'),p.owner, p.name,
t.num_rows
order by
      1 asc;

--**************************************************
--   Index Report Section
--**************************************************

column nbr_scans   format 999,999,999
column num_rows    format 999,999,999
column tbl_blocks  format 999,999,999
column owner       format a9;
column table_name  format a20;
column index_name  format a20;

ttitle 'Index full scans and counts'
select
      to_char(sn.end_interval_time,'mm/dd/rr hh24') time,
      p.owner,
      d.table_name,
      p.name index_name,
      seg.blocks tbl_blocks,
      sum(s.executions_delta) nbr_scans
from
      dba_segments seg,
      dba_indexes d,
      dba_hist_sqlstat     s,
      dba_hist_snapshot sn,
```

```
   (select distinct
      p1.sql_id,
      object_owner owner,
      object_name name
   from
      dba_hist_sql_plan p1
   where
      operation = 'INDEX'
      and
      options = 'FULL SCAN') p
where
   d.index_name = p.name
   and
   s.snap_id = sn.snap_id
   and
   s.sql_id = p.sql_id
   and
   d.table_name = seg.segment_name
   and
   seg.owner = p.owner
having
   sum(s.executions_delta) > 9
group by
   to_char(sn.end_interval_time,'mm/dd/rr hh24'),p.owner,
d.table_name, p.name, seg.blocks
order by
   1 asc;

ttitle 'Index range scans and counts'
select
   to_char(sn.end_interval_time,'mm/dd/rr hh24') time,
   p.owner,
   d.table_name,
   p.name index_name,
   seg.blocks tbl_blocks,
   sum(s.executions_delta) nbr_scans
from
   dba_segments seg,
   dba_hist_sqlstat     s,
   dba_hist_snapshot sn,
   dba_indexes d,
   (select distinct
      p1.sql_id,
      object_owner owner,
      object_name name
   from
      dba_hist_sql_plan p1
   where
      operation = 'INDEX'
      and
      options = 'RANGE SCAN') p
where
   d.index_name = p.name
   and
   s.snap_id = sn.snap_id
   and
   s.sql_id = p.sql_id
```

```
   and
   d.table_name = seg.segment_name
   and
   seg.owner = p.owner
having
   sum(s.executions_delta) > 9
group by
   to_char(sn.end_interval_time,'mm/dd/rr hh24'),p.owner,
d.table_name, p.name, seg.blocks
order by
   1 asc;

ttitle 'Index unique scans and counts'
select
   to_char(sn.end_interval_time,'mm/dd/rr hh24') time,
   p.owner,
   d.table_name,
   p.name index_name,
   sum(s.executions_delta) nbr_scans
from
   dba_hist_sqlstat    s,
   dba_hist_snapshot sn,
   dba_indexes d,
   (select distinct
     pl.sql_id,
     object_owner owner,
     object_name name
   from
      dba_hist_sql_plan pl
   where
     operation = 'INDEX'
     and
     options = 'UNIQUE SCAN') p
where
   d.index_name = p.name
   and
   s.snap_id = sn.snap_id
   and
   s.sql_id = p.sql_id
having
   sum(s.executions_delta) > 9
group by
   to_char(sn.end_interval_time,'mm/dd/rr hh24'),p.owner,
d.table_name, p.name
order by
   1 asc;

spool off
```

Once the problem was identified, it was easily fixed by the creation of three materialized views and the employment of a query rewrite which reduced physical disk I/O by over 2,000

percent. This process improved performance by more than 30x -
a real silver bullet!

With the release of version 10g, the Oracle database has never
been better for the management of very large databases. Some
favorite new features are the ability to track SQL execution over
time and to employ Oracle partitioning, materialized views, and
start transformation joins for super-fast data access.

Conclusion

This chapter has focused on the Oracle performance issues
related to very large Database (VLDB) systems. The main points
of this chapter include:

- The Oracle parallel query is a critical component of databases
  where very-large tables must be accessed via full-table scans.

- Materialized Views are an extremely important tool for pre-
  joining tables and pre-summarizing frequently referenced
  data.

- Decision Support Systems are very different from OLTP
  systems, and Oracle will often perform parallel large-table-
  full-table scans, making data buffers less important.

The next chapter provides a detailed examination of the finest
silver bullet of all, the Oracle index.

Indexing Silver Bullets

Don't get burned by unnecessary large-table full-table scans.

Indexes: The Ultimate Silver Bullet

Indexes are one of the best silver bullets. The addition of missing indexes or the improvement of index selectivity with function-based indexes can improve the efficiency of thousands of SQL statements.

There are many ways to apply indexes as a silver bullet in Oracle:

- **Add Missing Indexes** - Identifying unnecessary large-table full-table scans from the *v$sql_plan* view or the *dba_hist_sqlplan* table will allow the quick location and employment of new indexes.

- **Improve Index Selectivity** - Logical I/O for SQL statements can be reduced by matching the most restrictive predicate in the WHERE clause with a function-based or standard b-tree index.

- **Implement Bitmap Indexes** - For tablespaces in read-only mode and low-update tables, bitmap indexes can greatly improve the performance of certain types of queries.

Fishing for Opportunity

The first step in seeking indexing opportunities is to go fishing in the library cache using the *v$sql_plan* view and locate large-table full-table scans.

The DBA can then drill-down and see if the large-table full-table scans are legitimate, or if the full-scan access can be replaced with an index.

This chapter will focus on the importance of understanding the *clustering_factor* and understanding the circumstances under which an index should be used.

Tuning SQL Execution with *clustering_factor*

With each new release of Oracle, the cost-based optimizer (CBO) improves. The most current enhancement with Oracle9i is that during the formulation of an execution plan, consideration is given to external influences such as CPU cost and I/O cost. As release Oracle10g evolved, even more improvements were evident in the ability of the CBO to always get the optimal execution plan for a query; however, the DBA still needs to understand the indexing mechanism.

Rules for Oracle Indexing

In order to understand how Oracle formulates an execution plan for a query, it is important to first know the rules Oracle uses when it determines whether to use an index.

The most important characteristics of column data are the clustering factor for the column and the selectivity of column values, even though other important characteristics within tables are known to the CBO. A column called *clustering_factor* in the *dba_indexes* view offers information on how the table rows are synchronized with the index. When the clustering factor is close to the number of data blocks, the column value is not row-ordered. When the *clustering_factor* approaches the number of rows in the table, the table rows are synchronized with the index.

To illustrate this, consider the following query that filters the result set using a column value:

```
select customer_name
from customer
where customer_state = 'New Mexico';
```

An index scan is faster for this query if the percentage of customers in New Mexico is small and the values are clustered on the data blocks. The decision to use an index versus a full-table scan is at least partially determined by the percentage of customers in New Mexico.

So, why would a CBO choose to perform a full-table scan when only a small number of rows are retrieved? Four factors synchronize to help the CBO determine whether to use an index or a full-table scan:

- the selectivity of a column value

- the *db_block_size*

- the *avg_row_len*

- the cardinality.

An index scan is usually faster if a data column has high selectivity and a low *clustering_factor* as shown in Figure 6.1.

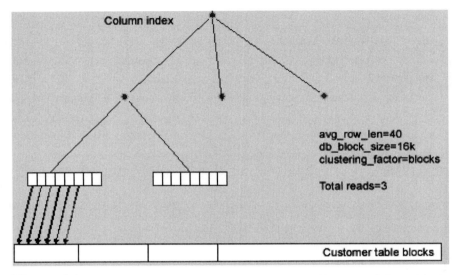

Figure 6.1: *Column with low clustering factor, small rows and large blocks.*

If a database has a frequent query that performs large index-range scans, the table can be forced into the same order as the index. By maintaining row order and thereby removing sub-optimal full-table scans, some queries (e.g. multi-block index range scans) may run far faster by placing all adjacent rows in the same data block.

Table row order can be forced with a single-table table cluster or by reorganizing the table with the *create table as select* syntax, using the SQL *order by* clause to force the row order. This is especially important when a majority of the SQL references a column with a high *clustering_factor,* a large *db_block_size,* and a small *avg_row_len.*

Even when a column has high selectivity, a high *clustering_factor,* and a small *avg_row_len,* there is still an indication that column values are randomly distributed in the table, and that an additional I/O will be required to obtain the rows.

On the other hand, as the *clustering_factor* nears the number of rows in the table, the rows fall out of sync with the index. This high *clustering_factor,* in which the value is close to the number of rows in the table (*num_rows),* indicates that the rows are out of sequence with the index and an additional I/O may be required for multi-block index range scans.

An index range scan would cause a huge amount of unnecessary I/O as shown in Figure 6.2, thus making a full-table scan more efficient.

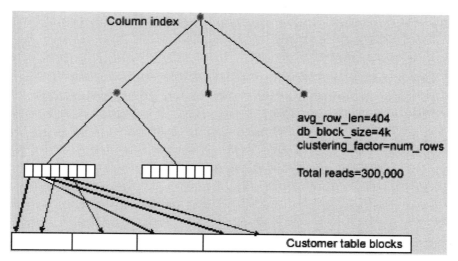

Figure 6.2: *Column with high clustering factor small blocks and large rows.*

The CBO's choice to execute a full-table versus an index range scan is influenced by the *clustering_factor*, *db_block_size*, and *avg_row_len*. Understanding how the CBO uses these statistics to determine the quickest way to deliver the desired rows is a noteworthy consideration.

The following section introduces a specialized type of index, the Oracle bitmap index. These types of indexes can hypercharge an Oracle database that has low update activity.

Implement Bitmap Indexes

There was a State Police query system was experiencing slow query performance. The system was read-only except for a 30-minute window at night for data loading. Inspection of the SQL showed complex combinational WHERE clauses like:

```
WHERE color='BLU' and make='CHEVY' and year=1997 and doors=2;
```

Concatenated indexes were used and the distinct values for each of these columns numbered less than 200. By replacing the b-tree indexes with bitmap indexes, the overall performance improvement of the system was incredible. Queries that had taken as much as three seconds to run were reduced to runtimes of under one-tenth of a second.

Adding Missing Indexes

When an Oracle Financial application shop called and reported that their performance degraded as more data was entered into the tables, a quick check of *v$sql_plan* using *plan9i.sql* script revealed several tables that had large-table full-table scans:

```
                         Full table scans and counts

OWNER      NAME                       NUM_ROWS  C  K    BLOCKS   NBR_FTS
---------- -------------------------  --------  -  -  --------   -------
APPLSYS    FND_CONC_RELEASE_DISJS       14,293  N          4,293  498,864
APPLSYS    FND_CONC_RELEASE_PERIODS    384,173  N         67,915  134,864
DONALD     PERSON_LOGON_ID          18,263,390  N        634,272   96,212
DONALD     SITE_AMDMNT               2,371,232  N         51,020   50,719
DONALD     CLIN_PTCL_VIS_MAP        23,123,384  N        986,395   11,273
```

The results indicate a huge number of large-table, full-table scans. Looking into *v$sql* revealed that the rows returned by each query were small, and a common WHERE clause for many queries looked like this:

```
WHERE customer_status = ':v1' and customer_age > :v2;
```

Creation of a concatenated index on CUSTOMER_STATUS and CUSTOMER_AGE resulted in a 50x performance improvement and a reduction in disk I/O by over 600 percent.

Another case for Missing Indexes

In a case utilizing an 8i database, the *access.sql* script below revealed suspect large-table, full-table scans:

```
                    Full table scans and counts

OWNER        NAME                  NUM_ROWS    C K   BLOCKS   NBR_FTS
----------   --------------------  ----------  - -   --------  --------
APPLSYS      FND_CONC_RELEASE_DISJS    1,293,292 N K   65,282    498,864
APPLSYS      FND_CONC_RELEASE_PERIODS  4,373,362 N K   62,282    122,764
APPLSYS      FND_CONC_RELEASE_STATES     974.193 N K    9,204     98,122
APPLSYS      FND_CONC_PP_ACTIONS         715,021 N      6,309     52,036
APPLSYS      FND_CONC_REL_CONJ_MEMBER     95,292 N K    4,409     23,122
```

Without knowing that Oracle 8i had new features to specifically address the issue, the DBA had created an index on the ORDER_DATE column only to discover that the *order_date* index was not being used. Creating the function-based index on *to_char(order_date,'MON-DD')* resulted in an immediate 5x performance improvement.

Conclusion

Oracle indexes are one of the best Silver Bullets because a single new index can improve the performance of thousands of SQL statements.

However, the use of Oracle indexes has some associated risk, and un-used indexes can slow-down DML (updates, deletes, inserts), and waste disk space.

Function-based indexes are one of the most powerful and under used Silver Bullets. The ability to match any WHERE clause criteria with an index can ensure that Oracle can get to the data rows with an absolute minimum of I/O.

The following section provides information on the 250+ Oracle init.ora parameters and gives helpful details on how changing a single parameter can have a Silver Bullet effect on a database.

Instance Parameter Silver Bullets

Carefully examine the many instance parameters

So Many Parameters!

Oracle considers its database system one of the world's most powerful and sophisticated and with that complexity also comes the flexibility to control aspects of data management. Oracle has hundreds of *init.ora* parameters that can often have a huge effect on the performance of an Oracle database.

If a DBA is using STATSPACK or AWR, then investigating and changing Oracle instance parameters becomes a simple task. The rules for instance tuning vary greatly, depending on the release of the Oracle database software. With each release, more of the initialization parameters become changeable via *alter system* commands. The following is a description of the distinctions between the different types of Oracle instance parameters.

Dynamic Instance Parameters

DBAs are concerned with proactive time-series tuning, so all dynamic parameters are ignored during the initial instance tuning. This is because ad-hoc triggers using *dbms_scheduler* can be created to change dynamic parameter values depending on database stress. Starting in Oracle9i, it became possible to adjust the values of several important SGA parameters:

- *shared_pool_size* - The memory region allocated for the library cache and internal control structures.

- *pga_aggregate_target* - A shared RAM area, outside the SGA, where Oracle performs sorting and hash joins.

- *db_cache_size* (and *db_2k_cache_size* . . . *db_32k_cache_size*) - The number of data buffers to allocate for the instance.

Oracle10g users can employ the Oracle10g Automatic Memory Management (AMM) facility for this area of instance tuning. Remember, the more processes that can be automated, the easier it will be to control time-based performance.

The following section is an introduction to non-changeable parameters.

Static Instance Parameters

The important parameters for instance tuning are those that are immutable, because they cannot be changed without starting and stopping the instance or using alter session commands and SQL hints. These parameters must be carefully set in order to accommodate the average load on the database. The most important of these parameters include:

- *db_file_multiblock_read_count* - When set to a high value, the CBO recognizes that scattered (multi-block) reads may be less expensive than sequential reads. This makes the CBO friendlier to full-table scans.

- *parallel_automatic_tuning* - When set to ON, full-table scans are parallelized. Since parallel full-table scans are very fast, the CBO will give a higher cost to index access and be friendlier to full-table scans.

- *optimizer_mode* - The optimal baseline setting for this parameter can affect the execution plans for thousands of SQL statements.

- *cursor_sharing* - The dynamic shop often has SQL that is generated by ad-hoc query tools with hard-coded literal values embedded within the SQL. Hard coded literal values make the SQL statements nonreusable unless *cursor_sharing=force* is set in the Oracle initialization file. Shops that are plagued with nonreusable SQL can adopt either the persistent or the dynamic philosophy. To use optimizer plan stability with nonreusable SQL, the DBA will set *cursor_sharing=force* and then extract the transformed SQL from the library cache and use optimizer plan stability to make the execution plan persistent.

- *optimizer_index_cost_adj* - This parameter controls the relative costs of full-table scans versus the index access cost. A lower value (20-30) makes indexes more attractive to the Oracle SQL optimizer.

- *optimizer_index_caching* - These parameters allows users to tell Oracle, on average, how many index blocks reside in the RAM data buffer cache. This is an important clue when the optimizer makes an access decision.

Please refer to Chapter 10, *Oracle SQL Silver Bullets* for complete information on SQL optimizer parameters. Optimizer statistics are important because this data collection is done at the instance level.

Oracle's Top Tuning Parameters

The following is Oracle MetaLink's list of the top performance parameters from MetaLink Note:223299.1.

The parameters listed below are new 9i parameters that affect database performance and should be tuned properly to get the optimal database performance.

- *cursor_sharing*
- *db_cache_size*
- *db_keep_cache_size*
- *db_recycle_cache_size*
- *db_16k_cache_size*
- *db_2k_cache_size*
- *db_32k_cache_size*
- *db_4k_cache_size*
- *db_8k_cache_size*
- *db_cache_advice*
- *pga_aggregate_target*
- *sga_max_size*
- *statistics_level*
- *workarea_size_policy*

Now that the parameters have been introduced, it will be helpful to examine how instance parameters can be changed in order to affect Oracle performance.

All about SGA RAM

All databases have a working set of frequently accessed table and index blocks that should always reside inside the data buffers for maximum performance.

This was a huge problem in 32-bit Oracle databases and servers with a RAM shortage. Oracle introduced the *v$db_cache_advice* utility and Oracle 10g Automatic Memory Management (AMM) to address this problem.

The total SGA size was historically difficult to grow beyond 1.7 GB without special tricks like Address Windowing Extension (AWE) and other operating-system tricks. It is still common to see databases on dedicated servers with 8 GB RAM with an SGA size of less than 500MB. Initiating an increase in SGA by increasing *db_block_buffers* or *db_cache_size* can dramatically improve performance.

Using the Oracle SGA Advisors

Oracle has introduced new advisory utilities and many of them are incorporated into the Oracle10g Automatic Memory Management (AMM) facility.

- **Data Cache Advice** - The new *v$db_cache_advice* view is similar to an Oracle7 utility that also predicted the benefit of adding data buffers. The Oracle7 utility used the *x$kcbrbh* view to track buffer hits and the *x$kcbcbh* view to track buffer misses. There is no longer any way to get cache advice on Oracle8 since *db_block_lru_statistics* was made obsolete.

- **Shared Pool Advice** - This shared pool advisory functionality has been extended in Oracle9i release 2 to include a new advice called *v$shared_pool_advice*. There is talk of expanding the advice facility to all SGA RAM areas in future releases of Oracle. Starting in Oracle9i release 2, *v$shared_pool_advice* shows the marginal difference in SQL parses as the shared pool changes in size from 10% of the current value to 200% of the current value.

- **PGA Target Advice** - Oracle AMM utilizes data from the *v$pga_target_advice* utility. This utility will show the marginal changes in optimal, one-pass, and multipass PGA execution for different sizes of *pga_aggregate_target*, ranging from 10% to 200% of the current value.

Standard Oracle STATSPACK and AWR reports also have reports from these advisors, and this data can be used to predict when to morph the SGA, before a performance issue is encountered.

RAM is an expensive database server resource, and the DBA has the responsibility to fully allocate RAM resources on the server. RAM that is not utilized wastes expensive hardware resources, and RAM depreciates regardless of usage.

When the marginal benefit of adding additional data blocks is plotted, the output looks like the following predictive model from *v$db_cache_advice:*

```
Size for  Size  Buffers for  Est Physical         Estimated
P   Estimate (M) Factr       Estimate  Read Factor  Physical Reads
--- ------------ -----       ---------- ------------ ----------------
D             88   .1           11,011       1.17     303,724,926
D            176   .2           22,022       1.08     279,266,295
D            264   .3           33,033       1.04     269,705,297
D            352   .4           44,044       1.03     267,659,834
D            440   .5           55,055       1.03     265,832,346  ← 50%
D            528   .6           66,066       1.02     264,201,407
D            616   .7           77,077       1.02     263,383,442
D            704   .8           88,088       1.01     262,127,570
D            792   .9           99,099       1.01     260,556,789
D            856  1.0          107,107       1.00     258,904,392  ← 100%
D            880  1.0          110,110       1.00     258,519,097
D            968  1.1          121,121       0.99     257,297,933
D          1,056  1.2          132,132       0.99     255,607,306
D          1,144  1.3          143,143       0.98     254,234,319
D          1,232  1.4          154,154       0.98     252,440,731
D          1,320  1.5          165,165       0.97     251,822,046
```

D	1,408	1.6	176,176	0.97	251,074,320	
D	1,496	1.7	187,187	0.97	249,856,517	
D	1,584	1.9	198,198	0.96	249,110,957	
D	1,672	2.0	209,209	0.70	182,328,040	← 200%
D	1,760	2.1	220,220	0.37	94,912,876	

When this data is plotted, the result is a typical 1/x curve. Figure 7.1 graphically shows that a marginal increase in data buffer blocks is asymptotic to disk I/O. A large reduction in disk I/O is achieved with a small increase in the size of a small RAM buffer.

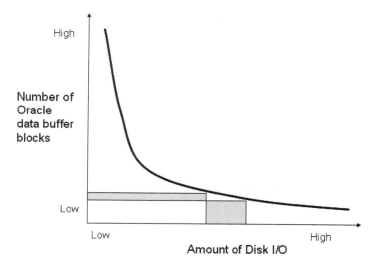

Figure 7.1: *Reduction in disk I/O from an increase to RAM data buffer.*

Here, a small increase in the size of *db_cache_size* results in a large reduction in actual disk I/O. This happens because the cache is small and frequently referenced data blocks are now able to stay resident in the RAM data buffer.

However, the impressive reduction in disk I/O does not continue indefinitely. As the total RAM size begins to approach the database size, the marginal reduction in disk I/O begins to decline as shown in Figure 7.2. This low marginal cost is due to the fact that all databases have data that is accessed infrequently. Infrequently accessed data does not normally have a bearing on the repeated reads performed by traditional OLTP applications, and this is why there is a marked decline in the marginal benefit as full RAM caching of the database is approached.

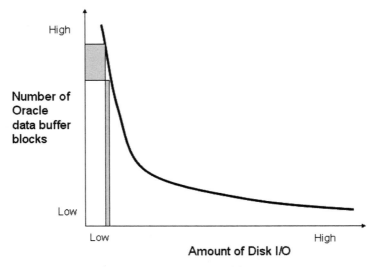

Figure 7.2: *Super-Large buffers result in small I/O gains.*

As a general guideline, all memory available on the host should be tuned, and the *db_cache_size* should be allocating RAM resources up to the point of diminishing returns as shown in Figure 7.3. This is the point where additional buffer blocks do not significantly improve the buffer hit ratio.

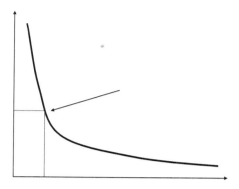

Figure 7.3: *The optimal size of the RAM data buffer.*

Bear in mind that the data buffer hit ratio can provide data similar to *v$db_cache_advice,* and most Oracle tuning professionals use both tools to monitor the effectiveness of their data buffers.

One of the most confounding problems with Oracle is the resolution of buffer busy wait events. Buffer busy waits are common in an I/O-bound Oracle system, as evidenced by any system with read (sequential/scattered) waits in the top-five waits in the Oracle STATSPACK or AWR reports, like this:

```
Top 5 Timed Events

                                                        % Total
  Event                         Waits        Time (s)   Ela Time
  ------------------------    -----------   ----------  ----------
  db file sequential read       2,598         7,146      48.54
  db file scattered read       25,519         3,246      22.04
  library cache load lock         673         1,363       9.26
  CPU time                      2,154           934       7.83
  log file parallel write      19,157           837       5.68
```

A common way to reduce buffer busy waits is to reduce the total I/O on the system. This can be done by tuning the SQL to access rows with fewer block reads (i.e., by adding indexes). Even if there is a huge *db_cache_size*, buffer busy waits may still exist, and increasing the buffer size won't help.

In order to look at system-wide wait events, the *v$system_event* performance view can be queried. This view, shown below, provides the name of the wait event, the total number of waits and timeouts, the total time waited, and the average wait time per event.

```
select *
from
   v$system_event
where
   event like '%wait%';
```

EVENT	TOTAL_WAITS	TOTAL_TIMEOUTS	TIME_WAITED	AVERAGE_WAIT
buffer busy waits	636528	1557	549700	.863591232
write complete waits	1193	0	14799	12.4048617
free buffer waits	1601	0	622	.388507183

The type of buffer that causes the wait can be queried using the *v$waitstat* view. This view lists the waits per buffer type for buffer busy waits, where COUNT is the sum of all waits for the class of block, and TIME is the sum of all wait times for that class.

```
select * from v$waitstat;
```

CLASS	COUNT	TIME
data block	1961113	1870278
segment header	34535	159082
undo header	233632	86239
undo block	1886	1706

Buffer busy waits occur when an Oracle session needs to access a block in the buffer cache but cannot because the buffer copy of the data block is locked. This buffer busy wait condition can happen for either of the following reasons:

- The block is being read into the buffer by another session, so the waiting session must wait for the block read to complete.

- Another session has the buffer block locked in a mode that is incompatible with the waiting session's request.

Because buffer busy waits are due to contention between particular blocks, there's nothing that can be done until the blocks that are in conflict have been identified along with why the conflicts are occurring. Tuning, therefore, involves identifying and eliminating the cause of the block contention.

If the top wait events query, as described above, reveals the fact that the wait event buffer busy waits has a large wait time, the *dba_hist_waitstat* view can be queried to investigate what particular type of block caused this situation.

For example, *dba_hist_active_sess_history* view can be queried to identify particular sessions and objects that caused the high contention. The datafile and objects ids can be found in the *v$session_wait* dynamic view. The following query can be used to retrieve historical block contention statistics:

wait_stat_int_10g.sql

```
-- *************************************************
-- Copyright © 2005 by Rampant TechPress
-- This script is free for non-commercial purposes
-- with no warranties.  Use at your own risk.
--
-- To license this script for a commercial purpose,
-- contact info@rampant.cc
-- *************************************************

select e.class "E.CLASS"
    , e.wait_count  - nvl(b.wait_count,0)      "Waits"
    , e.time        - nvl(b.time,0)            "Total Wait Time
(cs)"
    , (e.time       - nvl(b.time,0)) /
      (e.wait_count - nvl(b.wait_count,0)) "Avg Time (cs)"
  from dba_hist_waitstat b
    , dba_hist_waitstat e
 where b.snap_id        = &pBgnSnap
   and e.snap_id        = &pEndSnap
   and b.dbid           = &pDbId
   and e.dbid           = &pDbId
   and b.dbid           = e.dbid
```

```
   and b.instance_number = &pInstNum
   and e.instance_number = &pInstNum
   and b.instance_number = e.instance_number
   and b.class           = e.class
   and b.wait_count      < e.wait_count
order by 3 desc, 2 desc
```

The sample query output looks like the following, and the highest average wait events for the database are easy to identify. This script can be easily altered to show the top wait events for each snapshot period by joining into the *dba_hist_snapshot* table.

```
SQL> @wait_stat_int_10g.sql

E.CLASS            Waits Total Wait Time (cs) Avg Time (cs)
------------------ ----- -------------------- -------------
undo header           97                  121   1,24742268
file header block      2                  114           57
```

The output of the *wait_stat_int_10g.sql* script shows which particular buffer wait events play a significant role.

The WISE tool has a corresponding report named Buffer Waits Summary that generates time-series charts for the block contention statistics as shown in Figure 7.4.

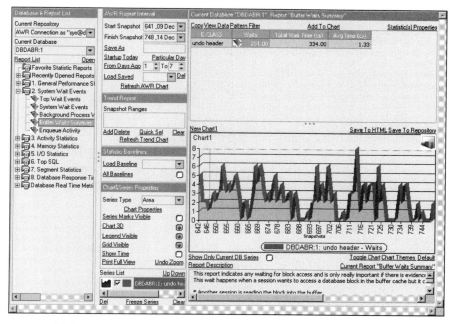

Figure 7.4: *AWR Buffer Waits Summary chart in WISE.*

The *v$session_wait* performance view can also give some insight into what is being waited for and why the wait is occurring.

The columns of the *v$session_wait* view that are of particular interest for a buffer busy wait event are:

- **P1** - The absolute file number for the data file involved in the wait.

- **P2** - The block number within the data file referenced in P1 that is being waited upon.

- **P3** - The reason code describing why the wait is occurring.

Here's an Oracle data dictionary query for these values:

```
select
 p1 "File #".
 p2 "Block #",
 p3 "Reason Code"
from
 v$session_wait
where
 event = 'buffer busy waits';
```

If the output from repeatedly running the above query shows that
a block or range of blocks is experiencing waits, the following
query should show the name and type of the segment:

```
select
 owner,
 segment_name,
 segment_type
from
 dba_extents
where
 file_id = &P1
and
 &P2 between block_id and block_id + blocks -1;
```

Once the segment is identified, the *v$segment_statistics* performance
view facilitates real time monitoring of segment-level statistics.
This enables a DBA to identify performance problems associated
with individual tables or indexes, as shown below.

```
select
   object_name,
   statistic_name,
   value
from
   V$SEGMENT_STATISTICS
where
   object_name = 'SOURCE$';

OBJECT_NAME    STATISTIC_NAME            VALUE
-----------    ------------------------  ----------
SOURCE$        logical reads             11216
SOURCE$        buffer busy waits         210
SOURCE$        db block changes          32
SOURCE$        physical reads            10365
SOURCE$        physical writes           0
SOURCE$        physical reads direct     0
SOURCE$        physical writes direct    0
SOURCE$        ITL waits                 0
```

The *dba_data_files* can be queried to determine the FILE_NAME for the file involved in the wait by using the P1 value from *v$session_wait* for the FILE_ID.

Buffer busy waits are prevalent in I/O-bound systems. I/O contention, resulting in waits for data blocks, is often due to numerous sessions repeatedly reading the same blocks, as when many sessions scan the same index.

In this scenario, session one scans the blocks in the buffer cache quickly, but then a block has to be read from disk. While session one waits for the disk read to complete, other sessions scanning the same index soon catch up to session one and want the same block currently being read from disk. This is where the buffer busy wait occurs-waiting for the buffer blocks that are being read from disk.

The following rules of thumb may be useful for resolving each of the noted contention situations:

- **Data Block Contention** - Identify and eliminate HOT blocks from the application via changing *pctfree* and or *pctused* values to reduce the number of rows per data block. Check for repeatedly scanned indexes. Since each transaction updating a block requires a transaction entry, increase the initrans value.

- **Freelist Block Contention** - Increase the freelists value. Also, when using RAC or OPS, be certain that each instance has its own FREELIST GROUPs.

- **Segment Header Contention** - Increasing the number of freelists or FREELIST GROUPs can relieve segment header contention and make DML run faster.

- **Undo Header Contention** - Increase the number of rollback segments.

The identification and resolution of buffer busy waits can be very complex and confusing. Oracle provides the *v$segment_statistics* view to help monitor buffer busy waits and the *v$system_event* views to identify the specific blocks for the buffer busy wait. While identifying and correcting the causes of buffer busy waits is not an intuitive process, the results can be quite rewarding.

Hidden Oracle Parameters

Each new release of Oracle brings new hidden (i.e., undocumented) parameters. These hidden parameters are sometimes used by internal Oracle development staff and are left inside Oracle for MetaLink emergency support. Many of these undocumented utilities are very powerful but can be complex.

Hidden initialization parameters are very dangerous because their use is undocumented, but they can be very valuable if the DBA is careful. If database links between Oracle instances on different versions of Oracle are used, an SQL*Plus query can be used to quickly find any new initialization parameters in a new version of Oracle:

```
select
   name
from
    v$parameter@oracle10g_instance
minus
select
   name
from
   v$parameter@oracle9i_instance
;
```

Every version of Oracle has special undocumented initialization parameters. These undocumented initialization parameters are usually only used in emergencies and only under the direction of a senior DBA or Oracle support. The undocumented parameters begin with an underscore "_", so a query against the *x$* foxed tables can be written to easily extract them:

hidden_parms.sql

```
--  *************************************************
--  Copyright © 2005 by Rampant TechPress
--  This script is free for non-commercial purposes
--  with no warranties.  Use at your own risk.
--
--  To license this script for a commercial purpose,
--  contact info@rampant.cc
--  *************************************************

COLUMN parameter              FORMAT a37
COLUMN description            FORMAT a30 WORD_WRAPPED
COLUMN "Session Value"        FORMAT a10
COLUMN "Instance Value"       FORMAT a10
SET LINES 100
SET PAGES 0
SPOOL undoc.lis

SELECT
    a.ksppinm  "Parameter",
    a.ksppdesc "Description",
    b.ksppstvl "Session Value",
    c.ksppstvl "Instance Value"
FROM
    x$ksppi a,
    x$ksppcv b,
    x$ksppsv c
WHERE
    a.indx = b.indx
    AND
    a.indx = c.indx
    AND
    a.ksppinm LIKE '/_%' escape '/'
/
```

Not everyone knows about the undocumented parameters and fewer know how or when to use them. Oracle does not allow DBAs to use many of these parameters unless specifically directed by Oracle support. DBAs should be aware that use of certain undocumented parameters is likely to result in a system that Oracle will not support.

In many cases, the undocumented parameters were either documented in previous releases or will be in future releases. Of course, it is difficult to use the undocumented parameters that have never been documented, and never will be, safely. When in doubt, get guidance from Oracle support.

Oracle makes a huge disclaimer that the undocumented initialization parameters are usually only used in emergencies. However, those who want to manipulate the internal mechanisms of Oracle to customize the behavior to their systems find the undocumented parameters very useful.

WARNING! Using undocumented parameters without the consent of Oracle can cause a system to be unsupported by Oracle. This leaves the DBAs on their own if data corruption is experienced. This is a serious warning!

With over 100 undocumented parameters, it is impossible to cover them all in this short book, so the following sections will focus on some of the most important parameters.

Many savvy Oracle professionals commonly adjust the hidden parameters to improve the overall performance of their systems. However, because these are considered undocumented parameters, most Oracle professionals rely on publications such as "Oracle Internals" to get insights into the proper setting for the hidden parameters.

Learning from Oracle Benchmarks

The www.tpc.org web site is a great place to find information on hidden Oracle parameters. Hardware vendors spend a fortune on their benchmarks and they must publish their Oracle parameters on this web site. For example, Hewlett-Packard announced a world record Oracle10g benchmark. Like most hardware vendors, HP took advantage of their Oracle hardware specific performance hidden parameters:

```
_in_memory_undo=false
_cursor_cache_frame_bind_memory = true
_db_cache_pre_warm = false
_in_memory_undo=false
_check_block_after_checksum = false
_lm_file_affinity
```

The following section offers quick survey of hidden Oracle parameters that are most likely to be silver bullets in a DBA shop.

Oracle Hidden Latch Parameters

Whenever index contention is experienced, as evidenced by process waits, adjusting the following parameters may be helpful.

- *_db_block_hash_buckets* - Defaults to 2 x *db_block_buffers* but should be the nearest prime number to the value of 2x *db_block_buffers*.

- *_db_block_hash_latches* - Defaults to 1024, but 32768 is a sometimes a better value.

- *_kgl_latch_count* - Defaults to zero. Lock contention can often be reduced by re-setting this value to 2*CPUs +1.

- *_latch_spin_count* - This parameter shows how often a latch request will be taken.

- *_db_block_write_batch* - Formerly documented, now undocumented. It is the number of blocks that the db writers will write in each batch. It defaults to 512 or *db_files*db_file_simultaneous_writes*/2 up to a limit of one-fourth the value of *db_cache_size*.

Oracle Parallel Query Parameters

The Oracle Parallel Query (OPQ) is an amazing facility for improving the speed of large-table full-table scans, and some DBAs are not aware that there are a dozen hidden parameters that can be changed to affect the behavior of parallel queries. The following query can be used to display the parameters:

opq_parms.sql

```
-- ***************************************************
-- Copyright © 2005 by Rampant TechPress
-- This script is free for non-commercial purposes
-- with no warranties.  Use at your own risk.
--
-- To license this script for a commercial purpose,
-- contact info@rampant.cc
-- ***************************************************

COLUMN parameter            FORMAT a37
COLUMN description          FORMAT a30 WORD_WRAPPED
COLUMN "Session VALUE"      FORMAT a10
COLUMN "Instance VALUE"     FORMAT a10
SET LINES 100 PAGES 0


SELECT
   a.ksppinm  "Parameter",
   a.ksppdesc "Description",
   b.ksppstvl "Session Value",
   c.ksppstvl "Instance Value"
FROM
   x$ksppi a,
   x$ksppcv b,
   x$ksppsv c
WHERE
   a.indx = b.indx
   AND
   a.indx = c.indx
   AND
   a.ksppinm LIKE '/_parallel%' escape '/'
;

SPOOL OFF
```

This script must be run from the SYS user as only the SYS user can access the *x$* internal tables. The following output shows the OPQ hidden parameters:

```
NAME                              VALUE
--------------------------------  -----------------------------
_parallel_adaptive_max_users      1
_parallel_default_max_instances   1
_parallel_execution_message_align FALSE
_parallel_fake_class_pct          0
_parallel_load_bal_unit           0
_parallel_load_balancing          TRUE
_parallel_min_message_pool        64560
_parallel_recovery_stopat         32767
_parallel_server_idle_time        5
_parallel_server_sleep_time       10
_parallel_txn_global              FALSE
_parallelism_cost_fudge_factor    350
```

The most important of these hidden parallel parameters is the *_parallelism_cost_fudge_factor*. This parameter governs the invocation of OPQ by the cost-based SQL optimizer when setting *parallel_automatic_tuning=true*. By adjusting this parameter the DBA can control the threshold for invoking parallel queries.

The following section presents information on some common DBA undocumented parameters. The following undocumented parameters are the most commonly used in Oracle administration.

Undocumented Parameters for Corruption Repair

These parameters allow the DBA to ignore corrupt data blocks when their database is corrupted. As a result, these parameters should only be used in emergencies.

- *_allow_resetlogs_corruption* - This parameter may be the only way to start a database that has been backed up open without setting backup on tablespaces. Use of this parameter will result in an unsupported system.

- _corrupted_rollback_segments_ - The only way to start up with corrupted public rollback segments. This undocumented parameter can be used without fear of invalidating support.

- _allow_read_only_corruption_ - This parameter allows the database to be opened even if it has corruption. This should only be used to export as much data from a corrupted database as is possible before recreating a database. A database that has been opened in this manner should not be used in a normal manner, as it will not be supported.

- _corrupt_blocks_on_stuck_recovery_ - This parameter can sometimes be useful for getting a corrupted database started. However, it probably won't be supported if it is used in this way without Oracle's blessing. Immediately export the tables needed and rebuild the database, if used.

SQL Optimizer Undocumented Parameters

These parameters control the internal behavior of the cost-based SQL optimizer (CBO).

- _fast_full_scan_enabled_ - This enables or disables fast full index scans, if only indexes are required to resolve the queries.

- _always_star_transformation_ - This parameter helps to tune data warehouse queries, provided that the warehouse is designed properly.

- _small_table_threshold_ - This sets the size definition of a small table. A small table is automatically pinned into the buffers when queried. This defaults to two percent in Oracle9i.

Data Buffer Behavior Parameters

For the very senior Oracle DBA, it is well understood that they can change the caching and aging rules within the Oracle _db_cache_size_ thereby changing the way that Oracle keeps data blocks in RAM memory. While these parameters are somewhat dangerous, some savvy DBAs have been able to get more efficient data caching by adjusting these values:

- *_db_aging_cool_count* - Controls the touch count set when buffer cooled.

- *_db_aging_hot_criteria* - Controls the touch count which sends a buffer to head of replacement list.

- *_db_aging_stay_count* - Controls the touch count set when buffer moved to head of replacement list.

- *_db_aging_touch_time* - Controls the touch count which sends a buffer to head of replacement list.

- *_db_block_hash_buckets* - Sets the number of database block hash buckets.

- *_db_block_hi_priority_batch_size* - Controls the fraction of writes for high priority reasons.

- *_db_block_max_cr_dba* - Defines the maximum Allowed Number of CR buffers per dba.

- *_db_block_max_scan_cnt* - Controls the maximum number of buffers to inspect when looking for free blocks.

- *_db_block_med_priority_batch_size* - Controls the fraction of writes for medium priority reasons.

Oracle undocumented parameters are especially useful to the senior Oracle DBA who needs to go beyond the recommended level of detail and wants to change the internal behavior of their SGA. The undocumented parameters are also a lifesaver for performing restarts of corrupted databases, but one must always remember that these parameters are hidden for a reason.

Oracle hidden parameters are very powerful and undocumented, so they should only be played with if there is a clear understanding about how they change the internal behavior of Oracle.

The following section provides an examination of some real world silver bullets that result from changes to the Oracle parameters.

Implement Cursor Sharing

There was an Oracle 9i database that had experienced poor performance immediately after a new manufacturing plant was added to the existing database. Since the AWR was not available in version 9.0.2, STATSPACK was used to isolate the top five timed events which looked like this:

```
Top 5 Wait Events
~~~~~~~~~~~~~~~~~~                                  Wait    % Total
Event                                   Waits   Time (cs)   Wt Time
--------------------------------------- ------------ ------------ -------
enqueue                                 25,901     479,654    46.71
db file scattered read              10,579,442     197,205    29.20
db file sequential read                724,325     196,583     9.14
latch free                           1,150,979      51,084     4.97
log file parallel write                148,932      39,822     3.88
```

A review of the SQL section of the STATSPACK report revealed that almost all of the SQL used literals in the WHERE clause of all queries.

```
WHERE customer_state = 'Alabama' and customer_type = 'REDNECK';
```

Using the *cursor_sharing* parameter was the only fast solution because the application was a vendor package with dynamically generated SQL. Setting *cursor_sharing=force* greatly reduced the contention on the library cache and reduced CPU consumption.

The end users reported a 75 percent improvement in overall performance.

Using the KEEP Pool

In an Oracle 9i system that had a 16 CPU Solaris server with 8GB of RAM, the client complained that performance had been degrading since the last production change. A STATSPACK top five timed events report showed that more than 80 percent of system waits were related to "db file scattered reads".

A quick review of *v$sql_plan* using *plan9i.sql* showed a number of small-table, full-table scans, with many of the tables not assigned to the KEEP pool. Tables assigned to the KEEP pool are denoted in the "K" column in the listing below:

```
                    Full table scans and counts

OWNER      NAME                   NUM_ROWS C K   BLOCKS  NBR_FTS
---------- ---------------------- -------- - - -------- --------
APPLSYS    FND_CONC_RELEASE_DISJS       39 N          44   98,864
APPLSYS    FND_CONC_RELEASE_PERIODS     39 N K        21   78,232
APPLSYS    FND_CONC_RELEASE_STATES       1 N K         2   66,864
APPLSYS    FND_CONC_PP_ACTIONS       7,021 N       1,262   52,036
APPLSYS    FND_CONC_REL_CONJ_MEMBER      0 N K       322   50,174
APPLSYS    FND_FILE_TEMP                 0 N         544   48,611
APPLSYS    FND_RUN_REQUESTS             99 N          98   48,606
INV        MTL_PARAMETERS                6 N K        16   21,478
APPLSYS    FND_PRODUCT_GROUPS            1 N          23   12,555
APPLSYS    FND_CONCURRENT_QUEUES_TL     13 N K        10   12,257
AP         AP_SYSTEM_PARAMETERS_ALL      1 N K         6    4,521
```

Rows fetched into the *db_cache_size* from full-table scans are not pinned to the Most Recently Used (MRU) end of the data buffer. Running a *buf_blocks.sql* script confirmed that the FTS blocks were falling off the least recently used end of the buffer and had to be frequently reloaded into the buffer.

```
                    Contents of Data Buffers
                                  Number of Percentage
                                  Blocks in of object
                 Object          Object   Buffer   Buffer  Buffer    Block
Owner            Name            Type     Cache    Blocks  Pool      Size
------------     ---------------  --------  --------  ------- ------- -------
DW01             WORKORDER       TAB PART  94,856        6 DEFAULT    8,192
DW01             HOUSE           TAB PART  50,674        7 DEFAULT   16,384
ODSA             WORKORDER       TABLE     28,481        2 DEFAULT   16,384
DW01             SUBSCRIBER      TAB PART  23,237        3 DEFAULT    4,096
ODS              WORKORDER       TABLE     19,926        1 DEFAULT    8,192
DW01             WRKR_ACCT_IDX   INDEX      8,525        5 DEFAULT   16,384
DW01             SUSC_SVCC_IDX   INDEX      8,453       38 KEEP      32,768
```

Therefore, running a *buf_keep_pool.sql* script to reassign all tables that experienced small-table, full-table scans into the KEEP pool was required. The output looks like the following and can be fed directly into SQL*Plus:

```
alter TABLE BOM.BOM_OPERATIONAL_ROUTINGS storage (buffer_pool keep);
alter INDEX BOM.CST_ITEM_COSTS_U1 storage (buffer_pool keep);
alter TABLE INV.MTL_ITEM_CATEGORIES storage (buffer_pool keep);
alter TABLE INV.MTL_ONHAND_QUANTITIES storage (buffer_pool keep);
alter TABLE INV.MTL_SUPPLY_DEMAND_TEMP storage (buffer_pool keep);
alter TABLE PO.PO_REQUISITION_LINES_ALL storage (buffer_pool keep);
alter TABLE AR.RA_CUSTOMER_TRX_ALL storage (buffer_pool keep);
alter TABLE AR.RA_CUSTOMER_TRX_LINES_ALL storage (buffer_pool keep);
```

In less than one hour, the problem was fixed via more efficient buffer caching, and overall database performance more than doubled.

Add Missing *init.ora* Parameters

There was a client who reported that system performance was growing progressively worse as more customers accessed the Oracle database. Upon examination, the *db_cache_size* parameter was not present in the *init.ora* file. A quick instance bounce to reset *sga_max_size* and *db_cache_size* resulted in a 400 percent performance improvement.

In one memorable case, a data warehouse client in California called and complained that performance degraded as the database grew. A quick study revealed the *sort_area_size* parameter was missing and defaulting to a tiny value. With a change of *sort_area_size=1048575* and a quick bounce of the instance, overall database performance improved by more than 50 percent.

Add Table Freelists

A frantic VP called and complained that the company's order processing center was unable keep up with new orders. The VP reported that 400 order entry clerks were experiencing 30-second response times and were forced to manually write down order information. It came to light that the client had just expanded the telephone order processing department and had doubled the order processing staff to meet a surge in market interest.

A *v$session* check found 450 connected users, and a quick scan of *v$sql* revealed that nearly all the Data Manipulation Locks (DML) were inserts into a *customer_order* table. The top timed event was *buffer busy wait* and it was clear that there were enqueues on the segment header blocks for the table and its indexes.

The next step in correcting this problem was to create a new tablespace for the table and index using Automatic Segment Space Management (ASSM), also known as bitmap freelists.

Once the ASSM tablespace is defined, the table can be reorganized online with the *dbms_redefinition* utility and then *alter index cust_pk* can be used to rebuild the index into the new tablespace.

In this situation, it would have taken several hours to build and execute the jobs and the VP said that he was losing over $500 per minute. Since the system was on release 9.2.0.4, it was easy to immediately relieve the segment header contention with the following commands:

```
alter table customer_order freelists 5;
alter index cust_pk freelists 5;
```

Without knowing the length of the enqueues on the segment header, it was necessary to add the additional freelists, one at a time until the buffer busy waits disappeared.

 The additional freelists were the key to the solution and the segment header contention disappeared.

This was only a stop-gap fix and as soon as the weekly purge was run, only one of the five freelists would get the released blocks which would cause the table to extend unnecessarily.

Conclusion

Oracle instance parameters govern every aspect of the Oracle configuration, and there are hundreds that can be used to improve the performance of an Oracle database. The main points of this chapter include:

- **SGA Parameters** - The parameters that control the sizes of the SGA regions are especially important to Oracle performance.

- **Optimizer Parameters** - The parameters that govern the behavior of the Oracle SQL optimizer can be a true silver bullet. Some parameters such as *optimizer_index_caching* are supposed to be set by the Oracle DBA.

- **Check the Benchmarks** - Use the www.tpc.org web site to see how Oracle experts configured their Oracle parameters for the fastest performance possible.

- **Use Hidden Parameters Cautiously** - Senior Oracle DBAs can get huge performance gains by adjusting the hidden parameters, but they must remember that they are not supported by Oracle. Any changes to undocumented parameters should be completely tested before using in a production instance.

The next chapter will present information on Oracle table structure silver bullets. The intelligent control of table structures can greatly improve database performance.

Table Structure Silver Bullets

Don't get stung by sub-optimal table definitions

Not all Tables are Created Equal

The correct use of Index-organized tables (IOT) and table clusters can greatly reduce both logical I/O (LIO) and physical I/O (PIO) by grouping related data rows together in adjacent data blocks.

To illustrate how resequencing can reduce both LIO and PIO and improve response times, consider a table in which the rows are not in the same sequence as the index. When the index is used to retrieve a series of rows that are adjacent to each other in the indexed version of the table, the index tree points to widely scattered locations among the physical blocks where the row data is stored. Figure 8.1 illustrates this concept.

Since the system must access many blocks to retrieve the data, it requires many I/O operations. If the table is resequenced, the rows will match the order of the primary-key index. Thus, the data from adjacent rows in the indexed table is stored in a single physical location on the disk, and I/O is reduced because the system needs to access fewer blocks in order to retrieve the data.

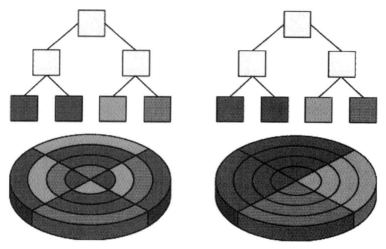

Figure 8.1: *Clustering rows to reduce I/O with index range scans.*

The degree to which resequencing improves performance depends on how far out of sequence the rows are when the process begins and how many rows will be accessed in sequence. How well a table's rows match the index's sequence key can be determined by looking at the *dba_indexes* and *dba_tables* views in the data dictionary. *dba_indexes* contains descriptions of all indexes in the database, and *dba_tables* contains descriptions of all relational tables in the database.

The *dbms_stats* package can be used to gather statistics. It is useful to remember that collecting statistics can affect optimizer behavior and severely degrade a system and that a large table can take some time to analyze.

In the *dba_indexes* view, the *clustering_factor* column will contain useful information. If the clustering factor, an integer, roughly matches the number of blocks in the table, the table is in sequence with the index order. However, if the clustering factor is close to the number of rows in the table, it indicates that the rows in the table are out of sequence with the index.

Indexes and Table Access

When deciding to segregate indexes into larger blocksizes, it is important to remember that those indexes subject to frequent "index range scans" will benefit the most from a larger blocksize.

When Oracle joins two tables together with a nested loop, only one of the indexes will be accessed. The optimizer always performs an index range scan on one index, gathers the rowid values, and then does fetch by rowid on the matching rows in the other table. For example:

```
select
    customer_name,
    order_date
from
    customer
    orders
where
    customer.cust_key = orders.cust_key;
```

Oracle will perform these steps to do the join, using the foreign key index:

- Index Range Scan the *order.cust_key* index and retrieve the customer rowid.

- Table access by ROWID for the matching customer rows.

If this nested loop never uses the customer index, why is it considered so useful? The answer is that it is used for index unique scans. In an index unique scan, a single row is accessed within the index. The following is an example of such a query:

```
select
   customer_last_name,
   customer_address
from
   customer
where
   cust_key = 123;
```

Some indexes are accessed with individual key values while others are accessed via index range scans as shown in Figure 8.2.

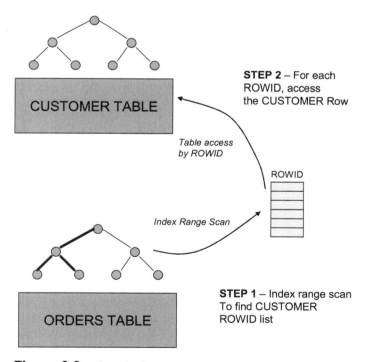

Figure 8.2: *Oracle does not always perform index range scans.*

An index that never experiences range scans would not benefit from a larger blocksize. The question then becomes one of finding those indexes that experience lots of range scans. The AWR can help this process.

Those indexes with the most index range scans can also be identified using this simple AWR script.

🖫 awr_sql_index_freq.sql

```
--  ****************************************************
-- Copyright © 2005 by Rampant TechPress
-- This script is free for non-commercial purposes
-- with no warranties.  Use at your own risk.
--
-- To license this script for a commercial purpose,
-- contact info@rampant.cc
--  ****************************************************

col c1 heading 'Object|Name'         format a30
col c2 heading 'Option'              format a15
col c3 heading 'Index|Usage|Count'   format 999,999

select
   p.object_name c1,
   p.options      c2,
   count(1)       c3
from
   dba_hist_sql_plan p,
   dba_hist_sqlstat  s
where
   p.object_owner <> 'SYS'
and
   p.options like '%RANGE SCAN%'
and

   p.operation like '%INDEX%'
and
   p.sql_id = s.sql_id
group by
   p.object_name,
   p.operation,
   p.options
order by
   1,2,3;
```

In the following output, the overall total counts for each object and table access method are shown.

```
                                            Index
Object                                      Usage
Name                        Option          Count
-------------------------   -------------   --------
CUSTOMER_CHECK              RANGE SCAN       4,232
AVAILABILITY_PRIMARY_KEY    RANGE SCAN       1,783
CON_UK                      RANGE SCAN         473
CURRENT_SEVERITY           RANGE SCAN         323
CWM$CUBEDIMENSIONUSE_IDX    RANGE SCAN          72
ORDERS_FK                   RANGE SCAN          20
```

This will quickly identify indexes that will benefit the most from a 32k blocksize.

This index list can be doubly verified by using AWR to identify indexes with high disk reads during each AWR snapshot period. The sample script below, *awr_top_tables_phyrd.sql,* exposes the top five tables accessed mostly heavily by physical disk reads for every snapshot interval:

💾 **awr_top_tables_phyrd.sql**

```
-- ************************************************
-- Copyright © 2005 by Rampant TechPress
-- This script is free for non-commercial purposes
-- with no warranties.  Use at your own risk.
--
-- To license this script for a commercial purpose,
-- contact info@rampant.cc
-- ************************************************

col c0 heading 'Begin|Interval|time'  format a8
col c1 heading 'Table|Name'           format a20
col c2 heading 'Disk|Reads'           format 99,999,999
col c3 heading 'Rows|Processed'       format 99,999,999

select
*
from (
select
    to_char(s.begin_interval_time,'mm-dd hh24') c0,
    p.object_name c1,
    sum(t.disk_reads_total) c2,
    sum(t.rows_processed_total) c3,
    DENSE_RANK() OVER (PARTITION BY
to_char(s.begin_interval_time,'mm-dd hh24') ORDER BY
SUM(t.disk_reads_total) desc) AS rnk
```

```
from
  dba_hist_sql_plan p,
  dba_hist_sqlstat t,
  dba_hist_snapshot s
where
  p.sql_id = t.sql_id
and
  t.snap_id = s.snap_id
and
  p.object_type like '%TABLE%'
group by
  to_char(s.begin_interval_time,'mm-dd hh24'),
  p.object_name
order by
c0 desc, rnk
)
where rnk <= 5
;
```

The following is a sample output from the above script:

Begin Interval time	Table Name	Disk Reads	Rows Processed	RNK
10-29 15	CUSTOMER_CHECK	55,732	498,056	1
10-29 15	CON_UK	18,368	166,172	2
10-29 15	CURRENT_SEVERITY	11,727	102,545	3
10-29 15	ORDERS_FK	5,876	86,671	4
10-29 15	SYN$	2,624	23,674	5
10-29 14	CUSTOMER_CHECK	47,756	427,762	1
10-29 14	CON_UK	15,939	142,878	2
10-29 14	CURRENT_SEVERITY	6,976	113,649	3
10-29 14	X$KZSRO	4,772	119,417	4
10-29 14	ORDERS_FK	2,274	20,292	5
10-29 13	CUSTOMER_CHECK	25,704	213,786	1
10-29 13	CON_UK	8,568	71,382	2
10-29 13	OBJ$	3,672	30,474	3

If there is a table that is almost always accessed via table access by rowid, the DBA may want to consider reorganizing the table into a hash cluster table.

Oracle Hash Cluster Tables

Oracle hash cluster tables can improve random row access speed by up to 4x because the hash can get the row location far faster than index access. Also, multiple table hash clusters can store logically-related rows on a single data block, allowing access to a whole unit of data in a single physical I/O.

Row Resequencing and Index Range Scans

Experienced Oracle DBAs know that I/O is often the single greatest component of response time. Disk I/O is expensive because when Oracle retrieves a block from a data file on disk, the reading process must wait for the physical I/O operation to complete.

Disk operations, physical reads, are about 100 times slower than a row's access in the data buffers, consistent gets. Consequently, anything that can be done to minimize I/O or reduce bottlenecks caused by contention for files on disk greatly improves the performance of any Oracle database.

If response times are lagging in a high-transaction system, reducing disk I/O is sometimes the best way to bring about a quick improvement. When tables are accessed in a transaction system exclusively through range scans in primary key indexes, reorganizing the tables with the CTAS method should be one of the first strategies used to reduce I/O. Like disk load balancing, row resequencing is easy, inexpensive, and relatively quick.

In high volume online transaction processing (OLTP) environments in which data is accessed via a primary index, re-sequencing table rows so that contiguous blocks follow the same order as their primary index can actually reduce physical I/O and improve response time during index-driven table queries. This technique is useful only when the application selects multiple rows, when using index range scans, or if the application issues multiple requests for consecutive keys. Databases with random primary key unique accesses won't benefit from row resequencing.

The following example illustrates how this works. Consider a SQL query that retrieves 100 rows using an index:

```
select
   salary
from
   employee
where
   last_name like 'B%';
```

This query will traverse the *last_name_index*, selecting each row to obtain the rows. This query will have at least 100 physical disk reads because the employee rows reside on different data blocks.

The same query can be resequenced such that the rows are in the same order as the *last_name_index*. The query can read all 100 employees with only three disk I/Os: one for the index; and two for the data blocks. This results in the savings of over 97 block reads.

The benefits of row resequencing cannot be underestimated. In large active tables with a large number of index scans, row resequencing can triple the performance of queries.

Once the decision to re-sequence the rows in a table has been made, one of the following tools can be used to reorganize the table:

- An Index-organized table.
- A single table index cluster table.
- The Oracle in-place table reorganization tool, *dbms_redefinition*.

The following section will focus on the most common methods for row resequencing for tables that are always accessed via index range scans.

Oracle Index Cluster Tables

Unlike the hash cluster where the symbolic key is hashed to the data block address, an index cluster uses an index to maintain row sequence.

A table cluster is a group of tables that share the same data blocks. This happens because they share common columns and are often used together. When cluster tables are created, Oracle physically stores all rows for each table in the same data blocks. The cluster key value is the value of the cluster key columns for a particular row.

Index cluster tables can be either multi-table or single-table.

Multi-Table Index Cluster Tables

In a multi-table index cluster, related table rows are grouped together to reduce disk I/O.

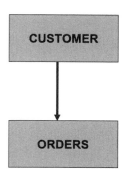

For example, assume that the database has a customer and orders table and 95% of the access is to select all orders for a particular customer.

Oracle will have to perform an I/O to fetch the customer row and then multiple I/O's to fetch each order for the customer.

Consider this SQL where all orders for a customer are fetched:

```
select
   customer_name,
   order_date
from
   customer
natural join
   orders
where
   cust_key = 'IBM';
```

If this customer has eight orders, each on a different data block, nine block fetches must be performed to return the query rows. Even if these blocks are already cached in the data buffers, there are still at least nine consistent gets:

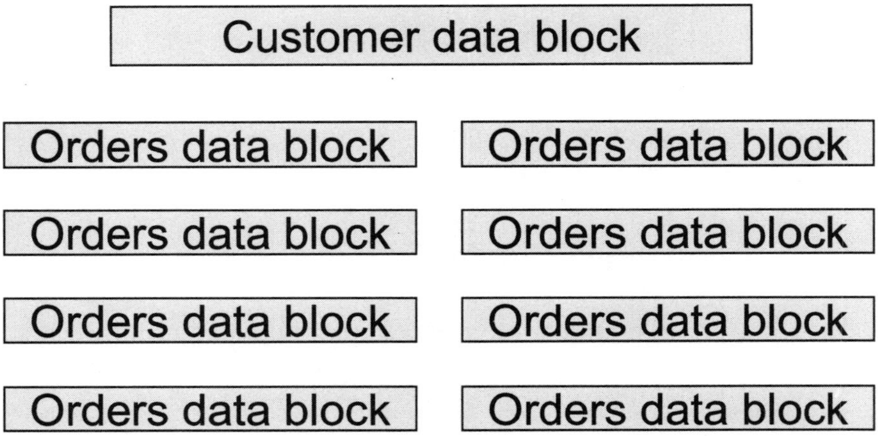

Customer data block

Orders data block	Orders data block
Orders data block	Orders data block
Orders data block	Orders data block
Orders data block	Orders data block

Figure 8.3: *Randomized data rows.*

If the table is redefined as an index cluster table, Oracle will physically store the orders rows on the same data block as the parent customer row, thereby reducing I/O by a factor of eight:

Order	Order	Order	Customer row	Order	Order	Order

Index clusters will only result in a reduction of I/O when the vast majority of data access is via the cluster index. Any row access via another index will still result in randomized block fetches.

Single-Table Index Cluster Tables

A single-table index cluster table is a method whereby Oracle guarantees row sequence where *clustering_factor* in *dba_indexes* always approximates *blocks* in *dba_tables*.

Scans via an index range scan will always fetch as many rows as possible in a single I/O, depending on the block size and average row length.

Many shops that employ single-table index cluster tables use a *db_32k_cache_size* to ensure that they can fetch an index range scan in a single I/O as shown in Figure 8.4.

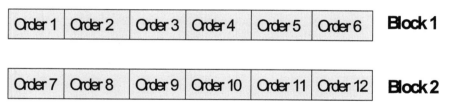

Figure 8.4: *Row sequencing with single-table index cluster tables.*

To do this, Oracle must have an overflow area where new rows are placed if there is not room on the target block. Monitoring the overflow becomes an important task and the DBA may have to periodically reorganize the single-table index cluster table to ensure that all row orders are maintained.

The DBA will lower the value of *pctfree* for the table to reserve space for new rows, but excessive row writes to the overflow area will cause the *clustering_factor* to rise above the value for blocks in *dba_tables* as shown in Figure 8.5.

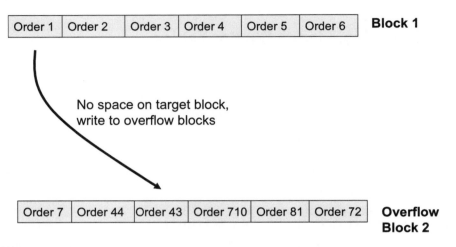

Figure 8.5: *An overflow area for a index table cluster.*

The type of table that has been defined can make a big difference in the amount of I/O required by Oracle to access the table rows.

Conclusion

This chapter has illustrated how the logical use of table structures can improve Oracle performance. The focus has been on the use of Oracle Index-organized tables (IOT), hash cluster tables and index cluster table structures.

The next step is to peel away another layer and examine the segment structures on disk, and find silver bullets that can be used there to improve Oracle performance.

Segment Structure Silver Bullets

Poor Disk I/O performance can be a major emergency.

It's All About I/O

Oracle databases are all about data retrieval and the job of the Oracle DBA is all about optimizing I/O. Whether the I/O is logical like a RAM buffer fetch or a physical disk read, the DBA must ensure that their Oracle database serves the queries with a minimum amount of work. Controlling the block sizes for specific tablespaces can help reduce stress on an Oracle database by making more efficient use of expensive RAM data buffers.

Many Oracle shops are plagued with slow I/O intensive databases, and this tip is for those who have AWR or

STATSPACK Top 5 timed events showing disk I/O as a major event:

```
Top 5 Timed Events
                                                     % Total
Event                      Waits       Time (s)    Ela Time
------------------------   ----------   ----------   ----------
db file sequential read     2,598        7,146        48.54
db file scattered read     25,519        3,246        22.04
library cache load lock       673        1,363         9.26
CPU time                    2,154          934         7.83
log file parallel write    19,157          837         5.68
```

This tip is important if read waits are among the top 5 timed events. If disk I/O is not the bottleneck, then making it faster will not improve performance.

Direct I/O is an OS-level solution, and often I/O-bound Oracle databases can be fixed by tuning the SQL to reduce unnecessary large-table full-table scans. The DBA then might monitor file I/O using the AWR *dba_hist_filestatxs* table or the STATSPACK *stats$filestatxs* table.

For optimal disk performance, Oracle should always use direct I/O to its data files, bypassing any caching at the OS layer. Direct I/O must be enabled both in Oracle and in the operating system.

Oracle and Direct I/O

This section is important if read waits are among the top 5 timed events of the database. If disk I/O is not the bottleneck, then making disk I/O faster WILL NOT improve performance.

For optimal disk performance, Oracle should always use direct I/O to its data files, bypassing any caching at the OS layer. This must be enabled both in Oracle and in the operating system.

Methods for configuring the disk I/O sub-system will vary depending on the operating system and file system that is being used; however, the DBA should always verify that I/O is optimized for the operating system.

The following are some examples of quick checks that anyone can perform to ensure that they are using direct I/O:

- **Solaris** - Look for a "forcedirectio" option. Oracle DBAs claim this option makes a huge difference in I/O speed for Sun servers.

- **AIX** - Look for a "dio" option

- **Veritas VxFS** (including HP-UX, Solaris and AIX) - look for "convosync=direct". It is also possible to enable direct I/O on a per file basis using Veritas QIO. Refer to the "qiostat" command and corresponding Man page for hints.

- **Linux** - Linux systems support direct I/O on a per filehandle basis. This process is much more flexible.

- **Windows** - Direct I/O is automatically enabled in Oracle10g at installation.

The next section presents a look at specific tools that the DBA can use to control their I/O sub-system.

The Debate about Oracle I/O Optimization

Oracle supports multiple blocksized tablespaces in a single database including 2k, 4k, 8k, 16k and 32k blocksizes.

There is debate about the benefit of different blocksizes (e.g. 8k, 32k) for the reduction of Oracle physical disk I/O and about

---

whether the Systems Administrator (SA) is likely to configure the Oracle server to use direct I/O for Oracle. This is not an issue for Oracle10g on Windows and Linux since they will always use direct I/O as the default.

Some SA's claim that placing large, related things (i.e. indexes) in a large blocksize results in a single physical fetch which requires less disk I/O. Other SA's report that this is not true because the OS blocksize and the JFS cache results in multiple I/Os at the operating system level.

According to Steve Adams, an extremely talented DBA and Oracle performance consultant, direct I/O and block size is a very important issue:

> It also avoids performance problems associated with using database block sizes that do not match the file system buffer size exactly.

Adams also notes that direct I/O can increase the size of the RAM available for the working set in the Oracle data buffers:

> By switching to raw or direct I/O and by giving Oracle the memory that would otherwise be used by the operating system to cache Oracle data, a much larger working set of data can be cached, and a much higher cache hit rate can be sustained with obvious performance benefits.

Oracle controls direct I/O with an initialization parameter named *filesystemio_options*. According to Steve Adams, the *filesystemio_options* parameter must be set properly in order for Oracle to read data blocks directly from disk:

> Databases that use a combination of say raw log files and raw tempfiles with file system based datafiles may wish to use kernelized asynchronous I/O against the raw files, but to avoid inefficient threaded asynchronous I/O against the datafiles.
>
> This can be done by allowing *disk_asynch_io* to default to TRUE, but setting *filesystemio_options* to either none or direct I/O.

While the configuration of the I/O sub-system is highly dependent on the OS and disk array product, there are some tools that the DBA can use to monitor and reduce unnecessary I/O.

Measuring File I/O with STATSPACK and AWR

One of the shortcomings of the old STATSPACK was that it could not directly monitor disk input and output (I/O) and statistics captured by a STATSPACK or AWR snapshot are related only to the read and write activity at the Oracle data file level. These statistics are stored in the *stats$filestatxs* or the *dba_hist_filestatxs* tables.

UNIX, on the other hand, displays read and write I/O statistics only at the physical disk level, and it is the responsibility of the Oracle administrator to know what mount points and disks are used to store the Oracle data files.

If DBA's segregate tables and indexes into separate tablespaces, they will know which objects reside in each file, and they can tell which tables and indexes are experiencing high I/O rates.

Measuring Specific Oracle I/O Activity

When the DBA prudently segregates Oracle objects into distinct datafiles and tablespaces, STATSPACK and the AWR can be used to create useful reports showing individual I/O, selected datafiles, or groups of related datafiles.

For example, the scripts below report on file-level I/O activity. If the largest and most important tables and indexes have purposely been segregated into separate data files, customer.dbf, custhistory.dbf, and custorders.dbf for example, then this script can be used to report the I/O history on all datafile names.

STATSPACK I/O Scripts

If STATSPACK is used with versions Oracle8i through Oracle9i, the following script will accept a specific filename and report on file level I/O:

🖫 **snapfileio_filename.sql**

```
--  ****************************************************
-- Copyright © 2005 by Rampant TechPress
-- This script is free for non-commercial purposes
-- with no warranties.  Use at your own risk.
--
-- To license this script for a commercial purpose,
-- contact info@rampant.cc
--  ****************************************************

set pages 9999;
column filename format a40
column mydate heading 'Yr. Mo Dy  ' format a16


select
  to_char(snap_time,'yyyy-mm-dd') mydate,
   sum(new.phyrds-old.phyrds)      phy_rds,
   sum(new.phywrts-old.phywrts)    phy_wrts
from
  perfstat.stats$filestatxs old,
  perfstat.stats$filestatxs new,
  perfstat.stats$snapshot    sn
where
```

```
  new.snap_id = sn.snap_id
and
  old.filename = new.filename
and
  old.snap_id = sn.snap_id-1
and
    (new.phyrds-old.phyrds) > 0
and
  old.filename like '%&1%'
group by
  to_char(snap_time,'yyyy-mm-dd'),
  old.filename;
```

The following is another version of this script, which sums the total I/O:

💾 snapfileio_sums.sql

```
-- *************************************************
-- Copyright © 2005 by Rampant TechPress
-- This script is free for non-commercial purposes
-- with no warranties.  Use at your own risk.
--
-- To license this script for a commercial purpose,
-- contact info@rampant.cc
-- *************************************************

rem
rem NAME: snapfileio.sql

rem FUNCTION: Reports on the file io status of all of the
rem FUNCTION: datafiles in the database for a single snapshot.


column sum_io1 new_value st1 noprint
column sum_io2 new_value st2 noprint
column sum_io new_value divide_by noprint
column Percent format 999.999 heading 'Percent|Of IO'
column brratio format 999.99 heading 'Block|Read|Ratio'
column bwratio format 999.99 heading 'Block|Write|Ratio'
column phyrds heading 'Physical | Reads'
column phywrts heading 'Physical | Writes'
column phyblkrd heading 'Physical|Block|Reads'
column phyblkwrt heading 'Physical|Block|Writes'
column filename format a45 heading 'File|Name'
column file# format 9999 heading 'File'

set feedback off verify off lines 132 pages 60 sqlbl on trims on

select
    nvl(sum(a.phyrds+a.phywrts),0) sum_io1
from
```

```
        stats$filestatxs a where snap_id=&&snap;
select nvl(sum(b.phyrds+b.phywrts),0) sum_io2
from
        stats$tempstatxs b where snap_id=&&snap;
select &st1+&st2 sum_io from dual;
rem
@title132 'Snap&&snap File I/O Statistics Report'
spool rep_out\&db\fileio&&snap

select
    a.filename, a.phyrds, a.phywrts,
    (100*(a.phyrds+a.phywrts)/&divide_by) Percent,
    a.phyblkrd, a.phyblkwrt, (a.phyblkrd/greatest(a.phyrds,1))
brratio,
       (a.phyblkwrt/greatest(a.phywrts,1)) bwratio
from
    stats$filestatxs a
where
    a.snap_id=&&snap
union
select
    c.filename, c.phyrds, c.phywrts,
    (100*(c.phyrds+c.phywrts)/&divide_by) Percent,
    c.phyblkrd, c.phyblkwrt,(c.phyblkrd/greatest(c.phyrds,1))
brratio,
       (c.phyblkwrt/greatest(c.phywrts,1)) bwratio
from
    stats$tempstatxs c
where
    c.snap_id=&&snap
order by
    1
/
spool off
pause Press enter to continue
set feedback on verify on lines 80 pages 22
clear columns
ttitle off
undef snap
```

The output from this script shows the total read and write activity per day for the datafiles. By viewing the output graphically, patterns of activity called I/O signatures can often be revealed. These signatures are useful in file load balancing.

```
Yr. Mo Dy          PHY_RDS    PHY_WRTS
----------------   --------   ---------
2002-12-18               7         226
2002-12-19              87         556
2002-12-20             141         640
2002-12-21              26         452
2002-12-22              45         368
2002-12-23              10         115
2002-12-24               3          14
2002-12-25               5          54
2002-12-26             169         509
2002-12-27              14         101
2002-12-28              25         316
2002-12-29              13         132
2002-12-30               7         158
2002-12-31               2         129
2003-01-01               4         264
2003-01-02              57         756
2003-01-03              56         317
2003-01-04            1110         123
2003-01-05            1075         386
2003-01-06              20         293
2003-01-07               1           6
2003-01-08             955        1774
2003-01-09             247        1145
2003-01-10             538        1724
2003-01-11             387        1169
2003-01-12            1017        1964
2003-01-13             115         397
2003-01-14              89         443
2003-01-15              22         125
2003-01-16            1267        1667
```

Free tools such as the MS-Excel chart wizard or a low-cost tool such as WISE can be used to visualize the I/O trends over time as shown in Figure 9.1.

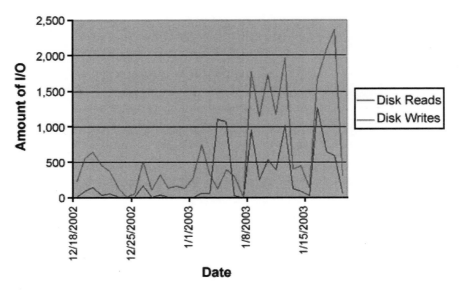

Figure 9.1: *Plotting Disk activity over time.*

Oracle 10g AWR I/O Scripts

Fortunately, tracking I/O is far simpler in Oracle10g. In Oracle10g, the AWR also provides the *dba_hist_filestatxs* table to track disk I/O. The following script uses the *dba_hist_filestatxs* table:

```
break on begin_interval_time skip 2
column phyrds format 999,999,999
column begin_interval_time format a25
select
   begin_interval_time,
   filename,
   phyrds
from
   dba_hist_filestatxs
natural join
   dba_hist_snapshot;
```

The following sample output shows physical I/O at the data file level:

```
BEGIN_INTERVAL_TIME        FILENAME                                          PHYRDS
-----------------------    ------------------------------------------     -----------
24-FEB-04 11.00.32.000 PM  E:\ORACLE\ORA92\FSDEV10G\SYSTEM01.DBF           164,700
                           E:\ORACLE\ORA92\FSDEV10G\UNDOTBS01.DBF           26,082
                           E:\ORACLE\ORA92\FSDEV10G\SYSAUX01.DBF           472,008
                           E:\ORACLE\ORA92\FSDEV10G\T_FS_LSQ.ORA             2,123
24-FEB-04 11.30.18.296 PM  E:\ORACLE\ORA92\FSDEV10G\SYSTEM01.DBF           167,809
                           E:\ORACLE\ORA92\FSDEV10G\UNDOTBS01.DBF           26,248
                           E:\ORACLE\ORA92\FSDEV10G\SYSAUX01.DBF           476,616
```

These are just a few of the available disk I/O scripts. www.oracle-script.com is one good source for scripts.

Now that the basic tools used to track disk I/O have been introduced, it's time to move on to an investigation of how the I/O sub-system can be adjusted.

Oracle Blocksize and Disk I/O

By now, the importance of multiple block sizes and multiple RAM caches should be clear. An understanding the salient issues surrounding block sizes enables the DBA to intelligently assign block sizes to tables and indexes.

"It looks like an I/O issue to me."

However, DBA's should also realize that tuning changes are never permanent, and they can experiment with different block sizes and the movement of tables from one tablespace to another. For example, if the I/O increases after a table is moved into a 2K tablespace, it can simply be moved into a larger sized tablespace. In the final analysis, minimizing I/O by adjusting block sizes is a long, iterative process.

The blocksize is especially important for Oracle indexes because the blocksize affects the b-tree structure and the amount of physical I/O required when fetching a rowid.

Oracle Blocksize and Index I/O

Within the Oracle index, each data block serves as a node in the index tree, with the bottom nodes (leaf blocks) containing pairs of symbolic keys and rowid values. Oracle controls the allocation of pointers within each data block to properly manage the blocks.

As an Oracle tree grows by the insertion of rows into the table, Oracle fills the block. When the block is full, it splits, creating new index nodes, also known as data blocks, to manage the symbolic keys within the index. Therefore, an Oracle index block may contain two types of pointers:

- rowid pointers to specific table rows.

- Pointers to other index nodes or data blocks.

The reason why a *pctused* value, the freelist re-link threshold, cannot be specified for indexes is because Oracle manages the allocation of pointers within index blocks. By studying an index block structure, it becomes apparent that the number of entries within each index node is a function of two values:

- The blocksize for the index tablespace.

- The length of the symbolic key.

The blocksize affects the number of keys within each index block; therefore, the blocksize will have an effect on the structure of the index tree. All else being equal, large 32K blocksizes will have more index keys, resulting in a flatter index structure.

In any event, there appears to be evidence that block size affects the tree structure, which supports the argument that the size of the data blocks affects the structure of the Oracle index tree.

To contain data from indexes or tables that are the object of repeated large scans, large (16K - 32K) blocksize data caches can be used. Does this actually help performance? A small but enlightening test can reveal the answer to that question. The following query for the test will be used against a 9i database that has a database block size of 8K but also has the 16K cache enabled along with a 16K tablespace:

```
select
      count(*)
from
      scott.hospital
where
      patient_id between 1 and 40000;
```

The SCOTT.HOSPITAL table has 150,000 rows and has an index build on the PATIENT_ID column. An explain plan of the query shows it uses an index range scan to manifest the desired end result:

```
Execution Plan
----------------------------------------------------------
0    SELECT STATEMENT Optimizer=CHOOSE
1      (Cost=41 Card=1 Bytes=4)
   1    0    SORT (AGGREGATE)
   2    1      INDEX (FAST FULL SCAN) OF 'HOSPITAL_PATIENT_ID'
               (NON-UNIQUE) (Cost=41 Card=120002 Bytes=480008)
```

Executing the query twice, to eliminate parse activity and to cache any data, with the index residing in a standard 8K tablespace produces these runtime statistics:

```
Statistics
---------------------------------------------------
          0  recursive calls
          0  db block gets
        421  consistent gets
          0  physical reads
          0  redo size
        371  bytes sent via SQL*Net to client
        430  bytes received via SQL*Net from client
          2  SQL*Net roundtrips to/from client
          0  sorts (memory)
          0  sorts (disk)
          1  rows processed
```

To quiz the competency of the new 16K cache and 16K tablespace, the index used by the query will be rebuilt into the 16K tablespace, which has the exact same aspects as the original 8K tablespace, except for the larger blocksize:

```
alter index
     scott.hospital_patient_id
     rebuild nologging noreverse tablespace indx_16k;
```

When the index is lodged firmly into the 16K tablespace, the query is executed again, twice, with the following runtime statistics being produced:

```
Statistics
---------------------------------------------------
          0  recursive calls
          0  db block gets
        211  consistent gets
          0  physical reads
          0  redo size
        371  bytes sent via SQL*Net to client
        430  bytes received via SQL*Net from client
          2  SQL*Net roundtrips to/from client
          0  sorts (memory)
          0  sorts (disk)
          1  rows processed
```

Simply by using the new 16K tablespace and accompanying 16K data cache, the amount of logical reads has been reduced by half. Most assuredly, the benefits of properly using the new data caches and multi-block tablespace feature of Oracle9i and later, are worth examination and trials in the DBA's own database.

Finding Hot Oracle Indexes

The *dba_hist_sql_plan* table can be used to gather counts about the frequency of participation of objects inside queries. This is a great query to quickly see what's going on between tables and the SQL that accesses them.

💾 **awr_sql_object_freq.sql**

```
-- **************************************************
-- Copyright © 2005 by Rampant TechPress
-- This script is free for non-commercial purposes
-- with no warranties.  Use at your own risk.
--
-- To license this script for a commercial purpose,
-- contact info@rampant.cc
-- **************************************************

col c1 heading 'Object|Name'          format a30
col c2 heading 'Operation'            format a15
col c3 heading 'Option'               format a15
col c4 heading 'Object|Count'         format 999,999

break on c1 skip 2
break on c2 skip 2

select
  p.object_name  c1,
  p.operation    c2,
  p.options      c3,
  count(1)       c4
from
   dba_hist_sql_plan p,
   dba_hist_sqlstat  s
where
   p.object_owner <> 'SYS'
and
   p.sql_id = s.sql_id
group by
   p.object_name,
   p.operation,
   p.options
order by
  1,2,3;
```

The following is the output where overall total counts for each object and table access method are shown.

Object Name	Operation	Option	Object Count
CUSTOMER	TABLE ACCESS	FULL	305
CUSTOMER _CHECK	INDEX	RANGE SCAN	2
CUSTOMER_ORDERS	TABLE ACCESS	BY INDEX ROWID	311
CUSTOMER_ORDERS		FULL	1
CUSTOMER_ORDERS_PRIMARY	INDEX	FULL SCAN	2
CUSTOMER_ORDERS_PRIMARY		UNIQUE SCAN	311
AVAILABILITY_PRIMARY_KEY		RANGE SCAN	4
CON_UK		RANGE SCAN	3
CURRENT_SEVERITY_PRIMARY_KEY		RANGE SCAN	1
CWM$CUBE	TABLE ACCESS	BY INDEX ROWID	2
CWM$CUBEDIMENSIONUSE		BY INDEX ROWID	2
CWM$CUBEDIMENSIONUSE_IDX	INDEX	RANGE SCAN	2
CWM$CUBE_PK		UNIQUE SCAN	2
CWM$DIMENSION_PK		FULL SCAN	2
MGMT_INV_VERSIONED_PATCH	TABLE ACCESS	BY INDEX ROWID	3
MGMT_JOB		BY INDEX ROWID	458
MGMT_JOB_EMD_STATUS_QUEUE		FULL	181
MGMT_JOB_EXECUTION		BY INDEX ROWID	456
MGMT_JOB_EXEC_IDX01	INDEX	RANGE SCAN	456
MGMT_JOB_EXEC_SUMMARY	TABLE ACCESS	BY INDEX ROWID	180
MGMT_JOB_EXEC_SUMM_IDX04	INDEX	RANGE SCAN	180
MGMT_JOB_HISTORY	TABLE ACCESS	BY INDEX ROWID	1
MGMT_JOB_HIST_IDX01	INDEX	RANGE SCAN	1
MGMT_JOB_PK		UNIQUE SCAN	458
MGMT_METRICS	TABLE ACCESS	BY INDEX ROWID	180

Using the output above, object participation, especially indexes, in the SQL queries and the mode an object was accessed by Oracle can be easily monitored.

Solutions to Physical Read Waits

Once the objects that experience the physical read waits have been identified, STATSPACK can be used to extract the SQL associated with the waits and the following actions taken to correct the problem. These corrective actions are presented in the order in which they are most likely to be effective, and some may not apply to a particular environment.

- **Tune the SQL Statement** - Tuning the SQL is the single most important factor in reducing disk I/O contention. If an SQL statement can be tuned to reduce disk I/O, the amount of disk I/O and associated waits are dramatically reduced.

- **Change the Table Join Order** - For sequential read waits, the SQL may be tuned to change the order that the tables are joined. This is often achieved using the ORDERED hint.

- **Change Indexes** - The SQL can be tuned by adding function-based indexes or using an INDEX hint to make the SQL less I/O-intensive by using a more selective index.

- **Change Table Join Methods** - Often, nested loop joins have fewer I/O waits than hash joins, especially for sequential reads. Table join methods can be changed with SQL hints (USE_NL, for example). If the database predates version Oracle9i with *pga_aggregate_target*, the propensity for hash joins can be changed by adjusting the *hash_area_size* parameter.

A database can also be tuned at the instance level with these techniques:

- **Get Better CBO Statistics** - Stale or non-representative statistics can cause suboptimal SQL execution plans, resulting in unnecessary disk waits. The solution is to use the *dbms_stats* package to analyze the schema. If column data values are skewed, adding histograms may also be necessary.

- **Distribute Disk I/O Across More Spindles** - Disk channel contention is often responsible for physical read waits, and they will show up in the ASH data. If disk waits are experienced as a result of hardware contention and RAID is not being used, consideration should be given to segregating the table of index into a separate tablespace with many data files and striping the offending data file across multiple disk spindles by reorganizing the object and using the minextents and next parameters.

- **Use the KEEP Pool** - Many experts recommend implementing the KEEP pool for reducing scattered reads. In the Oracle Magazine article "*Advanced Tuning with STATSPACK*" (Jan/Feb. 2003), the author notes that small-table full-table scans should be placed in the KEEP pool to reduce scattered read waits.

- **Increase the *db_cache_size*** - The more data blocks in the RAM buffer, the smaller the probability of physical read wait events.

The *dba_hist_sqltext* table keeps a record of historical SQL source statements and it is easy to extract the SQL that was executing at the time of the read waits. From there, the execution plans for the SQL statements can be gathered and it can be verified they are using an optimal execution plan.

The following section presents information on how multiple blocksizes can be used within Oracle databases to minimize I/O.

Multiple Blocksizes

Databases with multiple blocksizes have been around for more than 20 years. They were first introduced in the 1980's as a method to segregate and partition data buffers. Once Oracle adopted multiple blocksizes in Oracle9i in 2001, the database foundation for using multiple blocksizes was already a well tested and proven approach. Non-relation databases such as the CA IDMS/R network database have been using multiple blocksizes for nearly two decades.

It's interesting that Oracle introduced multiple blocksizes while not realizing their full potential. Originally implemented to support transportable tablespaces, Oracle DBA's quickly realized the huge benefit of multiple blocksizes for improving the utilization and performance of Oracle systems. These benefits fall into several general areas:

Multiple Blocksizes for Reducing Data Buffer Waste

By performing block reads of an appropriate size, the DBA can significantly increase the efficiency of the data buffers. For example, consider an OLTP database that randomly reads 80 byte customer rows. If a database has a 16k *db_block_size*, Oracle must read all of the 16k into the data buffer to get 80 bytes, a waste of data buffer resources.

If this customer table is migrated into a 2k blocksize, only 2k needs to be read-in to get the row data. This results in 8 times more available space for random block fetches as shown in Figure 9.2.

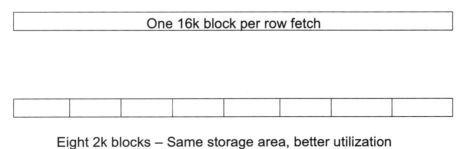

Figure 9.2: *Improvements in data buffer utilization.*

Multiple Blocksizes for Reducing Logical I/O

As more and more Oracle database become CPU-bound as the result of solid-state disks and 64-bit systems with large data buffer caches, minimizing logical I/O consistent gets from the data buffer has become an important way to reduce CPU consumption.

This can be illustrated with indexes. Oracle performs index range scans during many types of operations such as nested loop joins and enforcing row order for result sets with an ORDER BY clause. In these cases, moving Oracle indexes into large blocksizes can reduce both the physical I/O disk reads and the logical I/O buffer gets.

Robin Schumacher has proven in his book, *Oracle Performance Troubleshooting* (2003, Rampant TechPress) that Oracle b-tree indexes are built in flatter structures in 32k blocksizes.

A huge reduction in logical I/O is seen during index range scans and sorting within the TEMP tablespace because adjacent rows are located inside the same data block as shown in Figure 9.3.

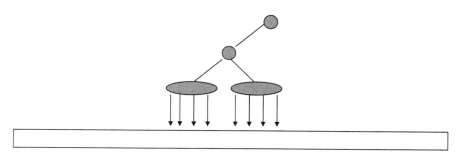

Index Range scan on 32k block – One consistent get

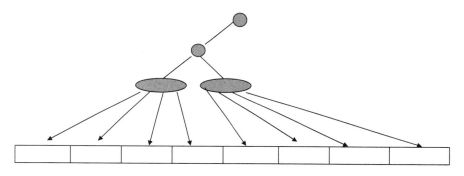

Index Range scan on 2k blocks – Eight consistent gets

Figure 9.3: *Improvements Logical I/O.*

Multiple Blocksizes for Improving Data Buffer Efficiency

One of the greatest problems of very large data buffers is the overhead of Oracle in cleaning out direct blocks that result from truncated operations and high activity DML. This overhead can drive up CPU consumption of databases that have large data buffers as shown in Figure 9.4.

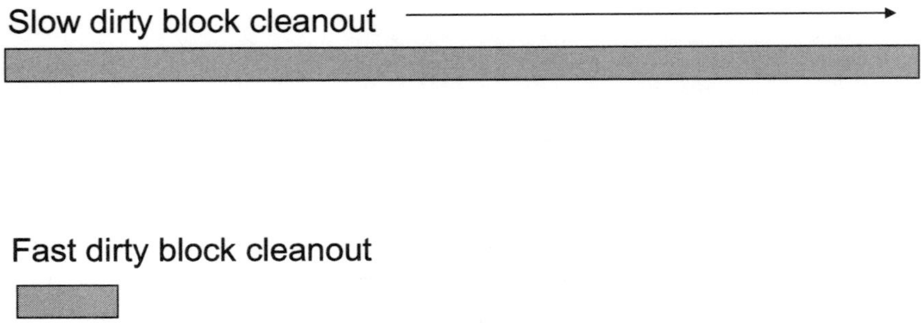

Slow dirty block cleanout $\longrightarrow$

Fast dirty block cleanout

Figure 9.4: *Dirty Block cleanup in a large vs. small data buffer.*

By segregating high activity tables into a separate, smaller data buffer, Oracle has far less RAM frames to scan for dirty blocks, improving the throughput and also reducing CPU consumption. This is especially important for update tables with more than 100 row changes per second.

Improving SQL Execution Plans

It's obvious that intelligent buffer segregation improves overall execution speed by reducing buffer gets, but there are also some other important reasons to use multiple blocksizes.

In general, the Oracle cost-based optimizer (CBO) is unaware of buffers details except when the *optimizer_index_caching* parameter is set. Using multiple data buffers will not impact SQL execution plans. When data using the new *cpu_cost* parameter in Oracle10g, the Oracle SQL optimizer builds the SQL plan decision tree based on the execution plan that will have the lowest estimated CPU cost.

For example, if a 32k data buffer is implemented for index tablespaces, the DBA can ensure that the indexes are caches for optimal performance and minimal logical I/O in range scans.

If an Oracle database has 50 gigabytes of index space, the DBA can define a 60 gigabyte *db_32k_cache_size* and then set *optimizer_index_caching* parameter to 100. This lets the SQL optimizer know that all of the Oracle indexes reside in RAM.

When Oracle makes the index versus table scan decision, knowing that the index nodes are in RAM will greatly influence the optimizer because the CBO knows that a logical I/O is often 100 times faster than a physical disk read.

In sum, moving Oracle indexes into a fully-cached 32k buffer will ensure that Oracle favors index access, reducing unnecessary full-table scans and greatly reducing logical I/O because adjacent index nodes will reside within the larger, 32k block.

Real World Applications of Multiple Blocksizes

The use of multiple blocksizes is most important for very large databases with thousands of updates per second and where thousands of concurrent users access terabytes of data. In these super-large databases, multiple blocksizes have proven to make a huge difference in response time.

The largest benefit of multiple blocksizes is seen in the following types of databases:

- **Large OLTP Databases** - Databases with a large amount of index access (*first_rows optimizer_mode*) and databases with random fetches of small rows are ideal for buffer pool segregation.

- **64-bit Oracle Databases** - Oracle databases with 64-bit software can support very large data buffer caches and these are ideal for caching frequently referenced tables and indexes.

- **High-Update Databases** - Databases where a small subset of the database receives large update activity (i.e. a single partition within a table), will see a large reduction in CPU consumption when the high update objects are moved into a smaller buffer cache.

However, there are specific types of databases that may not benefit from using multiple blocksizes:

- **Small Node Oracle10g Grid Systems** - Because each data blade in an Oracle10g grid node has only 2 to 4 gigabytes of RAM, data blade grid applications do not show a noticeable benefit from multiple block sizes.

- **Solid-State Databases** - Oracle databases using solid-state disks (RAM-SAN) perform fastest with super-small data buffer, just large enough to hold the Oracle serialization locks and latches.

- **Decision Support Systems** - Large Oracle data warehouses with parallel large-table full table scans do not benefit from multiple blocksizes. Parallel full-table scans bypass the data buffers and store the intermediate rows sets in the PGA region. As a general rule, databases with the *all_rows optimizer_mode* may not benefit from multiple blocksizes.

Even though Oracle introduced multiple blocksizes for an innocuous reason, their power has become obvious in very large database systems. The same divide-and-conquer approach that Oracle has used to support very large databases can also be used to divide and conquer Oracle data buffers.

Setting the *db_block_size* with Multiple Blocksizes

When multiple blocksizes are implemented, *db_block_size* or *db_cache_size* should be set based on the size of the tablespace where the large-object full-scans will be occurring. The parameter *db_file_multiblock_read_count* is only applicable for tables/indexes that are full scanned.

When multiple blocksizes are implemented, Oracle MetaLink notes that the *db_file_multiblock_read_count* should always be set to a value that sums to the largest supported blocksize of 32k:

db_block_size	db_file_multiblock_read_count
2k	16
4k	8
8k	4
16k	2

One issue with Oracle multiple block sizes is the setting for *db_file_multiblock_read_count* because this value influences the SQL optimizer about the costs of a full-table scan.

Objects that experience full scans or multi-block reads should be placed in a larger block size, with *db_file_multiblock_read_count* set to the block size of that tablespace.

According to Oracle, this is the formula for setting *db_file_multiblock_read_count*:

$$db\_file\_multiblock\_read\_count = \frac{max\ I/O\ chunk\ size}{db\_block\_size}$$

What is the maximum I/O chunk size? The maximum effective setting for *db_file_multiblock_read_count* is OS and disk dependant.

Steve Adams, an independent Oracle performance consultant (see www.ixora.com.au), has published a helpful script to assist in setting an appropriate level.

🖫 multiblock_read_test.sql

```
-- ************************************************
-- Copyright © 2005 by Rampant TechPress
-- This script is free for non-commercial purposes
-- with no warranties.  Use at your own risk.
--
-- To license this script for a commercial purpose,
-- contact info@rampant.cc
-- ************************************************


-----------------------------------------------------------------------
--
-- Script:    multiblock_read_test.sql
-- Purpose:   find largest actual multiblock read size
--
-- Copyright: (c) Ixora Pty Ltd
-- Author:    Steve Adams
--
-- Description:This script prompts the user to enter the name of a table to
--             scan, and then does so with a large multiblock read count, and
--             with event 10046 enabled at level 8.
--             The trace file is then examined to find the largest multiblock
--             read actually performed.
--
-----------------------------------------------------------------------

@save_sqlplus_settings

alter session set db_file_multiblock_read_count = 32768;
/
column value heading "Maximum possible multiblock read count"
select
  value
from
  sys.v_$parameter
where
  name = 'db_file_multiblock_read_count'
/


prompt
@accept Table "Table to scan" SYS.SOURCE$
prompt Scanning ...
set termout off
```

```
alter session set events '10046 trace name context forever, level 8'
/
select /*+ full(t) noparallel(t) nocache(t) */ count(*) from &Table t
/
alter session set events '10046 trace name context off'
/

set termout on


@trace_file_name


prompt
prompt Maximum effective multiblock read count
prompt ---------------------------------------

host sed -n '/scattered/s/.*p3=//p' &Trace_Name | sort -n | tail -1

@restore_sqlplus_settings
```

Conclusion

This chapter covered the minimization of I/O at the segment level and ensuring that the Oracle database fetches data with a minimum amount of I/O overhead. The main points of this chapter include:

- **Is the System I/O-Bound?** - If the database is not I/O constrained, speeding-up I/O may not help performance.

- **Use Direct I/O** - Make sure that the OS is configured for direct I/O to bypass the OS buffers and read the data directly into the Oracle data buffers.

- **Don't Waste Data Buffers** - Segregate objects according to their I/O patters and use multiple blocksizes to reduce I/O.

- **Watch the Configuration** - Several parameters such as *db_file_multiblock_read_count* are very important to the I/O sub-system.

The next chapter will present valuable information on one of the most important Silver Bullets, SQL tuning.

Oracle SQL Silver Bullets

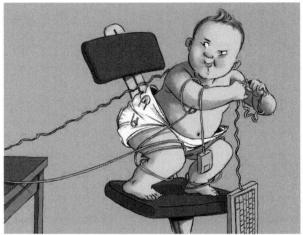

Some developers don't know that they can control SQL execution

Inside SQL Tuning

Most Oracle DBAs have very little control over the original SQL in their applications. Vendor applications and in-house systems where the developers are free to put SQL into a production database can be very frustrating for the tuning DBA.

SQL tuning by the DBA can be hindered in a variety of ways:

- **Vendor Packages** - Most vendors do not permit the alteration of their SQL statements.

- **Distributed SQL** - SQL that is kept inside client side applications is difficult to tune because of the problems distributing the SQL back to the clients.

- **Ad-hoc Queries** - Applications that permit ad-hoc queries (i.e. Crystal Reports) reply on the query generator to formulate efficient SQL.

- **Dynamic SQL** - SQL that is created dynamically within the application is especially hard to change.

Does this mean that the DBA is powerless to tune the SQL? Oracle provides a wealth of tools that allow the DBA to tune SQL:

- **Stored Outlines (SQL Profiles)** - Oracle has tools such as the Oracle optimizer plan stability and the Oracle10g SQL profiles to allow the DBA to change execution plans for SQL without touching the SQL source statement.

- **PL/SQL Procedures** - Smart shops that encapsulate SQL inside PL/SQL procedures allow the DBA to get the source for any SQL statements from the data dictionary and quickly tune the query.

- **Optimizer Parameters** - As presented in Chapter 7, *Instance Parameter Silver Bullets,* there are a host of parameters that allow the DBA to tune SQL execution.

- **Optimizer Statistics** - The DBA controls the most important part of SQL execution, the proper collection of CBO statistics. Although the statistics collection is automatic in Oracle10g, senior DBAs continue to tweak the statistics to improve SQL performance.

- **Indexes** - As noted in Chapter 6, Indexing Silver Bullets, indexes are a great tool for the Oracle DBA, especially function-based indexes.

The next logical step is a review of techniques and script that can be used to locate sub-optimal SQL statements.

The Goals of SQL Tuning

Despite the inherent complexity involved in the tuning of SQL, there are general guidelines that every Oracle DBA follows in order to improve the overall performance of their Oracle systems. The goals of SQL tuning are simple:

- Replace unnecessary large-table full table scans with index scans.

- Cache small-table full table scans.

- Verify optimal index usage.

- Verify optimal JOIN techniques.

The following section presents information on these goals and how they simplify SQL tuning.

Remove Unnecessary Large-Table Full Table Scans

Unnecessary full table scans (FTS) cause a huge amount of unnecessary I/O and can drag down an entire database. The tuning expert first evaluates the SQL based on the number of rows returned by the query. Oracle documentation states that a query return of less than 40 percent of the table rows in an ordered table or seven percent of the rows in an unordered table, based on the index key value described by *clustering_factor* in *dba_indexes*, the query can be tuned to use an index in lieu of the full table scan.

However, it's not that simple. The speed of a FTS versus an index scan depends on many factors:

- Missing indexes, especially function-based indexes.

- Bad/stale CBO statistics.

- Missing CBO Histograms.

- Clustering of the table rows to the used index.

The most common tuning for unnecessary full table scans is adding indexes, especially function-based indexes. The decision about removing a full table scan should be based on a careful examination of the amount of logical I/O consistent gets of the index scan versus the costs of the full table scan, factoring in the multiblock reads and possible parallel full-table scan execution.

In some cases, an unnecessary full table scan can be forced to use an index by adding an index hint to the SQL statement.

Cache Small-Table Full Table Scans

Cases in which a full table scan is the fastest access method, the tuning professional should ensure that a dedicated data buffer is available for the rows. In Oracle7, a alter table xxx cache command can be issued. In Oracle8 and beyond, the small table can be cached by forcing it into the KEEP pool.

Logical read consistent gets are often 100x faster than a disk read and small, frequently-referenced tables and indexes should be fully cached in the KEEP pool.

- Check *x$bh* periodically and move any table that has 80% or more of its blocks in the buffer into the KEEP pool.

- Check *dba_hist_sqlstat* for tables that experience frequent small-table full-table scans.

Verify Optimal Index Usage

This is especially important for improving the speed of queries with multiple WHERE clause predicates. Oracle sometimes has a choice of indexes, and the tuning professional must examine each index and ensure that Oracle is using the best index which is the one that returns the result with the least consistent gets.

Verify Optimal JOIN Techniques

Some queries will perform faster with NESTED LOOP joins; some with HASH joins, while others favor SORT-MERGE joins. It is difficult to predict prior to trying each one exactly what join technique will be fastest, so many Oracle tuning experts will test run the SQL with each different table join method.

These methods may seem deceptively simple, but these tasks comprise 90 percent of SQL tuning, and do not require a thorough understanding of the internals of Oracle SQL. The following sections present an overview of the Oracle SQL optimizers.

Of course, DBA's can tune the SQL all they want, but if they do not feed the optimizer with the correct statistics, the optimizer may not make the correct decisions. Before starting the tuning process, it is important to have current statistics available.

Some believe in the practice of running statistics at a preset schedule, such as weekly for example. Some believe in just calculating statistics when the data changes. Still others believe that statistics are only run to fix a poor access path, and once things are good; they should not be touched. Since all approaches work to some degree based on the situation, it is difficult to say which is correct.

Therefore, the features in Oracle 10g that notifies the DBA when statistics are old and need to be recalculated are extremely helpful. Gone are the days when statistics were calculated weekly, or on whatever schedule, just in case the data changed. There is now certainty, one way or the other. Of course, some will still believe new statistics should only be calculated if the database is having a problem, and once decent access paths have been established, the database should be left alone.

Before moving on to the tuning of individual SQL statements, the following section will examine how global Oracle parameters and features influence SQL execution.

Oracle SQL Performance Parameters

The Cost-based Optimizer (CBO) is not psychic despite the definition of the word oracle. In database terms, Oracle can never know the exact load on the Oracle system prior to its initial use; therefore, the Oracle professional must adjust the CBO behavior periodically.

Most Oracle professionals make these behavior adjustments using the instance-wide CBO behavior parameters such as *optimizer_index_cost_adj* and *optimizer_index_caching*. However, Oracle does not advise altering the default values for many of these CBO settings because the changes can affect the execution plans for thousands of SQL statements.

Some primary adjustable parameters that influence the behavior of the CBO are shown below:

- *parallel_automatic_tuning* - Full-table scans are parallelized when set to ON. Since parallel full-table scans are extremely quick, the CBO will give a higher cost to index access and will be friendlier to full-table scans.

- *hash_area_size* (if not using *pga_aggregate_target*) - The setting for the *hash_area_size* parameter governs the propensity of the CBO to favor hash joins over nested loops and sort merge table joins.

- *db_file_multiblock_read_count* - The CBO, when set to a high value, recognizes that scattered (multi-block) reads may be less expensive than sequential reads. This makes the CBO friendlier to full-table scans.

- *optimizer_index_cost_adj* - This parameter controls the CBO's propensity to favor index scans over full-table scans. It changes the costing algorithm for access paths involving indexes. The smaller the value, the cheaper the cost of index access.

- *optimizer_index_caching* - This parameter informs Oracle of the amount of space the index is likely to require in the RAM data buffer cache. The setting for *optimizer_index_caching* affects the CBO's decision to use an index for a table join (nested loops) or to favor a full-table scan.

- *optimizer_max_permutations* - This controls the maximum number of table join permutations allowed before the CBO is forced to pick a table join order. For a six-way table join, Oracle must evaluate 6 factorial (6!), or 720 possible join orders for the tables. This parameter has been deprecated in Oracle10g.

- *sort_area_size* (if not using *pga_aggregate_target*) - The *sort_area_size* influences the CBO when analyzing whether to perform an index access or a sort of the result set. The higher the value for *sort_area_size*, the more likely a sort will be performed in RAM, and the more likely that the CBO will favor a sort over presorted index retrieval.

In a dynamic system, as the type of SQL and load on the database changes, the ideal value for some parameters may change radically in just a few minutes. One important Oracle parameter that this applies to is the *optimizer_index_cost_adj* parameter. The next section examines the importance of this parameter.

Using *Optimizer_index_cost_adj*

One important Oracle parameter is the *optimizer_index_cost_adj*, and the default setting of 100 is not the optimum setting for most Oracle systems. For OLTP systems, resetting this parameter to a smaller value (between 10 and 30) may result in huge performance gains as SQL statements change from large-table full-table scans to index range scans. The Oracle environment can be queried in order to intelligently estimate the optimal setting for *optimizer_index_cost_adj*.

The *optimizer_index_cost_adj* parameter defaults to a value of 100 and can range in value from one to 10,000. A value of 100 means that equal weight is given to index versus multiblock reads. In other words, *optimizer_index_cost_adj* can be thought of as a "how cheap is a full-table scan?" parameter.

With the default value of 100, the CBO sometimes costs full-table scans too low. A number lower than 100 informs the CBO that index scans are less costly than full-table scans. Although, even at the lowest setting (*optimizer_index_cost_adj*=1), the CBO will still choose full-table scans for no-brainers such as tiny tables that reside on two blocks.

💾 optimizer_index_cost_adj.sql

```
-- *************************************************
-- Copyright © 2005 by Rampant TechPress
-- This script is free for non-commercial purposes
-- with no warranties.  Use at your own risk.
--
-- To license this script for a commercial purpose,
-- contact info@rampant.cc
-- *************************************************

col c1 heading 'Average Waits for|Full Scan Read I/O'     format 9999.999
col c2 heading 'Average Waits for|Index Read I/O'         format 9999.999
col c3 heading 'Percent of| I/O Waits|for Full Scans'     format 9.99
col c4 heading 'Percent of| I/O Waits|for Index Scans'    format 9.99
col c5 heading 'Starting|Value|for|optimizer|index|cost|adj' format 999
```

```
select
   a.average_wait                               c1,
   b.average_wait                               c2,
   a.total_waits /(a.total_waits + b.total_waits)  c3,
   b.total_waits /(a.total_waits + b.total_waits)  c4,
   (b.average_wait / a.average_wait)*100        c5
from
   v$system_event  a,
   v$system_event  b
where
   a.event = 'db file scattered read'
and
   b.event = 'db file sequential read'
;
```

The following is the output from the script:

				Starting Value for optimizer index cost adj
Average waits for full scan read I/O	Average waits for index read I/O	Percent of I/O waits for full scans	Percent of I/O waits for index scans	
1.473	.289	.02	.98	20

In this example, the suggested starting value of 20 for *optimizer_index_cost_adj* may be too high because 98 percent of the data waits are on index (sequential) block access. Weighting this starting value for *optimizer_index_cost_adj* to reflect the reality that this system has only two percent waits on full-table scan reads, which would indicate a typical OLTP system with few full-table scans, is a practical matter. An automated value for *optimizer_index_cost_adj* should never be less than one or more than 100.

Now that the processes have been introduced, at the next section will introduce some handy scripts that can be used for locating bad SQL.

Finding the Problem SQL Sessions

Even if a DBA is not using a database monitor that offers a "Top Sessions" view, the SQL that is giving a database grief can still be easily pinpointed. In truth, different database professionals have their own ideas about what constitutes a Top Session.

Some feel that the sum total of physical I/O alone tells the story, while others look at CPU, and still others use a combination of physical and logical I/O. Whatever the DBA's individual preference, the following script can be used to quickly bubble to the top twenty sessions in an Oracle9i database. Note that the initial sort is on physical I/O, but this can be changed to be any other column desired.

🔲 top_20_sessions.sql

```
-- ********************************************************
-- Copyright © 2005 by Rampant TechPress
-- This script is free for non-commercial purposes
-- with no warranties.  Use at your own risk.
--
-- To license this script for a commercial purpose,
-- contact info@rampant.cc
-- ********************************************************
select * from
(select b.sid sid,
     decode (b.username,null,e.name,b.username) user_name,
     d.spid os_id,
     b.machine machine_name,
     to_char(logon_time,'dd-mon-yy hh:mi:ss pm') logon_time,
   (sum(decode(c.name,'physical reads',value,0)) +
    sum(decode(c.name,'physical writes',value,0)) +
    sum(decode(c.name,'physical writes direct',value,0)) +
    sum(decode(c.name,'physical writes direct (lob)',value,0))+
    sum(decode(c.name,'physical reads direct (lob)',value,0)) +
    sum(decode(c.name,'physical reads direct',value,0)))
    total_physical_io,
   (sum(decode(c.name,'db block gets',value,0)) +
    sum(decode(c.name,'db block changes',value,0)) +
    sum(decode(c.name,'consistent changes',value,0)) +
    sum(decode(c.name,'consistent gets',value,0)) )
    total_logical_io,
   (sum(decode(c.name,'session pga memory',value,0))+
    sum(decode(c.name,'session uga memory',value,0)) )
    total_memory_usage,
    sum(decode(c.name,'parse count (total)',value,0)) parses,
    sum(decode(c.name,'cpu used by this session',value,0))
    total_cpu,
    sum(decode(c.name,'parse time cpu',value,0)) parse_cpu,
    sum(decode(c.name,'recursive cpu usage',value,0))
```

```
        recursive_cpu,
    sum(decode(c.name,'cpu used by this session',value,0)) -
    sum(decode(c.name,'parse time cpu',value,0)) -
    sum(decode(c.name,'recursive cpu usage',value,0))
        other_cpu,
    sum(decode(c.name,'sorts (disk)',value,0)) disk_sorts,
    sum(decode(c.name,'sorts (memory)',value,0)) memory_sorts,
    sum(decode(c.name,'sorts (rows)',value,0)) rows_sorted,
    sum(decode(c.name,'user commits',value,0)) commits,
    sum(decode(c.name,'user rollbacks',value,0)) rollbacks,
    sum(decode(c.name,'execute count',value,0)) executions
from sys.v_$sesstat a,
    sys.v_$session b,
    sys.v_$statname c,
    sys.v_$process d,
    sys.v_$bgprocess e
where a.statistic#=c.statistic# and
    b.sid=a.sid and
    d.addr = b.paddr and
    e.paddr (+) = b.paddr and
    c.NAME in ('physical reads',
                'physical writes',
                'physical writes direct',
                'physical reads direct',
                'physical writes direct (lob)',
                'physical reads direct (lob)',
                'db block gets',
                'db block changes',
                'consistent changes',
                'consistent gets',
                'session pga memory',
                'session uga memory',
                'parse count (total)',
                'CPU used by this session',
                'parse time cpu',
                'recursive cpu usage',
                'sorts (disk)',
                'sorts (memory)',
                'sorts (rows)',
                'user commits',
                'user rollbacks',
                'execute count'
)
group by b.sid,
        d.spid,
        decode (b.username,null,e.name,b.username),
        b.machine,
        to_char(logon_time,'dd-mon-yy hh:mi:ss pm')
order by 6 desc)
where rownum < 21
```

The above query can also be modified to exclude Oracle
background processes such as the SYS and SYSTEM user, etc.
The end result should be a current list of the top offending

sessions in the database as ranked by various performance metrics, which is the normal way to rank problem user accounts. The following is a sample output of this query.

SID	USER...	OS_ID	MACHINE...	LOGON_TIME	TOTAL_PH...	TOTAL_L...	TOTAL_MEM...
132	SYSM...	2040	lstcha2003	01-dec-04 ...	3.00	1134191.00	955168.00
146	SYSM...	1396	lstcha2003	03-dec-04 ...	35.00	21789.00	1045600.00
162	SYSM...	1396	lstcha2003	03-dec-04 ...	16.00	1769.00	700880.00
144	SYSM...	1396	lstcha2003	01-dec-04 ...	6.00	1333527.00	768180.00
140	SYSM...	1396	lstcha2003	01-dec-04 ...	439.00	3223273...	1586080.00
149	SYSM...	1396	lstcha2003	01-dec-04 ...	46.00	3062974.00	1004972.00
142	SYSM...	1396	lstcha2003	01-dec-04 ...	37.00	228448.00	1110892.00
133	SYSM...	1396	lstcha2003	01-dec-04 ...	21.00	299.00	602468.00
131	SYSM...	1396	lstcha2003	01-dec-04 ...	15.00	527.00	783800.00
134	SYSM...	1396	lstcha2003	01-dec-04 ...	189.00	8359.00	1069060.00
151	SPV	688	LEAVES\LS...	17-dec-04 ...	80.00	7154.00	584972.00
165	SMON	992	LSTCHA2003	23-nov-04 ...	1210.00	4144932.00	978188.00
164	RECO	1004	LSTCHA2003	23-nov-04 ...	1.00	3425.00	519436.00
158	MMON	412	LSTCHA2003	23-nov-04 ...	402.00	3157815.00	5563116.00
167	LGWR	1704	LSTCHA2003	23-nov-04 ...	18.00	0.00	5106956.00
168	DBW0	556	LSTCHA2003	23-nov-04 ...	1775674.00	6.00	2272588.00
141	DBSN...	1632	LEAVES\LS...	23-nov-04 ...	220.00	3679438.00	1144416.00
166	CKPT	996	LSTCHA2003	23-nov-04 ...	2048.00	0.00	985708.00
163	CJQ0	1284	LSTCHA2003	23-nov-04 ...	65.00	1649981.00	912508.00
137		1268	LSTCHA2003	23-nov-04 ...	53.00	6436456.00	781436.00

DBAs know that a user's resource consumption is almost always tied to inefficient SQL, so they would like to cut to the chase and find the problem sessions in a database that have caused most of the large table scans on the system or have submitted queries containing Cartesian joins. The *v$sql_plan* view contains execution plan data for all submitted SQL statements. Such a view provides a wealth of information regarding the performance and efficiency of SQL statements and the sessions that submitted them.

For example, if a DBA wants to know what sessions have parsed SQL statements that caused large, over one Megabyte, table scans on a system along with the total number of large scans, by session; the following query could be submitted:

🖫 high_scan_sql.sql

```
-- ************************************************
-- Copyright © 2005 by Rampant TechPress
-- This script is free for non-commercial purposes
-- with no warranties.  Use at your own risk.
--
-- To license this script for a commercial purpose,
-- contact info@rampant.cc
-- ************************************************

select
    c.username          username,
    count(a.hash_value) scan_count
from
    sys.v_$sql_plan  a,
    sys.dba_segments b,
    sys.dba_users    c,
    sys.v_$sql       d
where
    a.object_owner (+) = b.owner
and
    a.object_name (+) = b.segment_name
and
    b.segment_type IN ('TABLE', 'TABLE PARTITION')
and
    a.operation like '%TABLE%'
and
    a.options = 'FULL'
and
    c.user_id = d.parsing_user_id
and
    d.hash_value = a.hash_value
and
    b.bytes / 1024 > 1024
group by
    c.username
order by
    2 desc
;
```

The output from the above query might look something like the following:

```
USERNAME    SCAN_COUNT
----------  ----------
SYSTEM              14
SYS                 11
ERADMIN              6
ORA_MONITOR          3
```

In like fashion, if a DBA wants to uncover what sessions have parsed SQL statements containing Cartesian joins along with the number of SQL statements that contain such joins, the following query could be used:

```
select
    username,
    count(distinct c.hash_value) nbr_stmts
from
    sys.v_$sql a,
    sys.dba_users b,
    sys.v_$sql_plan c
where
    a.parsing_user_id = b.user_id
and
    options = 'CARTESIAN'
and
    operation like '%JOIN%'
and
    a.hash_value = c.hash_value
group by
    username
order by
    2 desc
;
```

A result set from this query could look similar to the following:

```
USERNAME    NBR_STMTS
---------   ---------
SYS                 2
SYSMAN              2
ORA_MONITOR         1
```

The *v$sql_plan* view adds more meat to the process of identifying problem sessions in a database. When combined with the standard performance metrics query, DBAs can really begin to pinpoint the sessions that are wreaking havoc inside their critical systems.

Identify the Resource-Intensive SQL

Since SQL comes to the Oracle database from external programs, the Oracle DBA must continually monitor the library cache for untuned SQL. After identifying the top resource hogging sessions in a database, attention can then be turned to the code they and others are executing that is likely causing system bottlenecks. As with Top Session monitors, many decent database monitors have a "Top SQL" feature that can help ferret out bad SQL code. In the absence of such tools, a script like the one shown below can be used.

🖫 **high_resource_sql.sql**

```
-- ****************************************************
-- Copyright © 2005 by Rampant TechPress
-- This script is free for non-commercial purposes
-- with no warranties.  Use at your own risk.
--
-- To license this script for a commercial purpose,
-- contact info@rampant.cc
-- ****************************************************

select sql_text,
       username,
       disk_reads_per_exec,
       buffer_gets,
       disk_reads,
       parse_calls,
       sorts,
       executions,
       rows_processed,
       hit_ratio,
       first_load_time,
       sharable_mem,
       persistent_mem,
       runtime_mem,
       cpu_time,
       elapsed_time,
       address,
       hash_value
from
(select sql_text ,
       b.username ,
 round((a.disk_reads/decode(a.executions,0,1,
 a.executions)),2)
       disk_reads_per_exec,
       a.disk_reads ,
```

```
        a.buffer_gets ,
        a.parse_calls ,
        a.sorts ,
        a.executions ,
        a.rows_processed ,
        100 - round(100 *
        a.disk_reads/greatest(a.buffer_gets,1),2) hit_ratio,
        a.first_load_time ,
        sharable_mem ,
        persistent_mem ,
        runtime_mem,
        cpu_time,
        elapsed_time,
        address,
        hash_value
from
    sys.v_$sqlarea a,
    sys.all_users b
where
    a.parsing_user_id=b.user_id and
    b.username not in ('sys','system')
order by 3 desc)
where rownum < 21
```

This script will pull the top twenty SQL statements as ranked by disk reads per execution. The ROWNUM filter can be changed at the end to show more or all SQL that has executed in a database. WHERE predicates can also be added that only show the SQL for one or more of the top sessions previously identified.

In Oracle9i, Oracle has added the CPU_TIME and ELAPSED_TIME columns, which provide more data that can be used to determine the overall efficiency of an SQL statement. The following is a sample output of this query:

SQL_TEXT	USERI	DISK_REA	BUFFER_GETS	DISK_READS	PARS	SORTS
update lob$ set retention = :1 where retention >= 0	SYS	791	1005	791	1	0
delete from sys.wri$_optstat_histgrm_history where s.	SYS	759	846	759	1	0
delete from WRH$_SYSMETRIC_SUMMARY tab w	SYS	691	7172	691	1	0
delete from WRH$_WAITCLASSMETRIC_HISTOR'	SYS	630	11132	630	1	0
delete from WRH$_SQL_PLAN tab where (:beg_sn	SYS	533	3743	533	1	0
delete from wrh$_sqltext tab where (tab.dbid = :dbid	SYS	522	1196	522	1	0
BEGIN prvt_advisor.delete_expired_tasks; END;	SYS	454	1424	454	1	0
begin dbms_feature_usage_internal.exec_db_usage	SYS	453	433868	453	1	0
delete from WRH$_ENQUEUE_STAT tab where (:t	SYS	427	10306	427	1	0
SELECT T.ID FROM WRI$_ADV_TASKS T, WRI$_	SYS	421	1133	421	1	0
select s.synonym_name object_name, o.object_type	SYS	397.5	434481	1590	4	0
select o.owner#,o.obj#,decode(o.linkname,null, dec:	SYS	362.5	6051	725	2	0
select atc + ix, NULL, NULL from (select count(*) atc	SYS	296	293988	296	1	0
delete from sys.wri$_optstat_histhead_history where	SYS	231	292	231	1	0
delete from WRH$_BG_EVENT_SUMMARY tab wt	SYS	207	6695	207	1	0
delete from WRI$_ALERT_HISTORY where time_st	SYS	188	2071	188	1	0
begin "SYS"."DBMS_REPCAT_UTL"."DROP_USE	SYS	163	4048	163	1	0
BEGIN ECM_CT.POSTLOAD_CALLBACK(:1, :2); EN	SYSM/	154	7904	308	2	0
begin "CTXSYS"."CTX_ADM"."DROP_USER_OBJ	SYS	118	2395	118	1	0
select table_objno, primary_instance, secondary_inst	SYS	111	688	111	1	0

The *v$sql_plan* view can also help with identification of problem SQL. For example, a DBA may want to know how many total SQL statements are causing Cartesian joins on a system. The following query can answer that question:

```
select
    count(distinct hash_value) carteisan_statements,
    count(*)                   total_cartesian_joins
from
    sys.v_$sql_plan
where
    options = 'CARTESIAN'
and
    operation like '%JOIN%'
```

Noting that it is possible for a single SQL statement to contain more than one Cartesian join, the output from this query may resemble the following:

```
CARTESIAN_STATEMENTS    TOTAL_CARTESIAN_JOINS
----------------------- ----------------------
                   3                        3
```

A DBA can then view the actual SQL statements containing the Cartesian joins, along with their performance metrics by using a query like the following:

```
--  **************************************************
-- Copyright © 2005 by Rampant TechPress
-- This script is free for non-commercial purposes
-- with no warranties.  Use at your own risk.
--
-- To license this script for a commercial purpose,
-- contact info@rampant.cc
--  **************************************************

select *
from
   sys.v_$sql
where
   hash_value in
      (select hash_value
       from
          sys.v_$sql_plan
       where
          options = 'CARTESIAN'
          and
          operation LIKE '%JOIN%' )
order by hash_value;
```

Another area of interest for DBAs is table scan activity. Most DBAs don't worry about small table scans because Oracle can many times access small tables more efficiency through a full scan than through index access. Large table scans, however, are another matter. Most DBAs prefer to avoid them where possible through smart index placement or intelligent partitioning.

Using the *v$sql_plan* view, a DBA can quickly identify any SQL statement that contains one or more large table scans. The following query shows any SQL statement containing a large, again greater than one Megabyte, table scan, along with a count of how many large scans it causes for each execution, the total number of times the statement has been executed, and the sum total of all scans it has caused on the system:

```
-- ***************************************************
-- Copyright © 2005 by Rampant TechPress
-- This script is free for non-commercial purposes
-- with no warranties.  Use at your own risk.
--
-- To license this script for a commercial purpose,
-- contact info@rampant.cc
-- ***************************************************

select
     sql_text,
     total_large_scans,
       executions,
       executions * total_large_scans sum_large_scans
from
(select
       sql_text,
       count(*) total_large_scans,
       executions
 from
       sys.v_$sql_plan a,
       sys.dba_segments b,
       sys.v_$sql c
 where
       a.object_owner (+) = b.owner
   and
       a.object_name (+) = b.segment_name
   and
       b.segment_type IN ('TABLE', 'TABLE PARTITION')
   and
       a.operation LIKE '%TABLE%'
   and
       a.options = 'FULL'
   and
       c.hash_value = a.hash_value
   and
       b.bytes / 1024 > 1024
   group by
      sql_text, executions)
order by
   4 desc
;
```

This query produces very interesting output as shown below. As a DBA, should the worry be more about an SQL statement that causes only one large table scan but has been executed 1000 times, or should a SQL statement that has ten large scans in it but has only been executed a handful of times?

	SQL_TEXT	TOTAL_LA	EXECUTIONS	SUM_LARGE_SCANS
1	select name,type#,obj#,remoteowner,linkname,namespace, subname from obj$ v ▦	1	71	71
2	select o.name,o.type#,o.obj#,o.remoteowner,o.linkname,o.namespace, o.subnam ▦	1	16	16
3	select object_name, object_type from sys.user_objects o where o.object_type in	▦	2	3	6
4	select s.synonym_name object_name, o.object_type from sys.all_synonyms s, ▦	1	4	4
5	select name, type#, obj#, remoteowner, linkname, namespace, subname from ob ▦	1	3	3
6	select object_name, object_type from sys.user_objects o where o.object_type in	▦	2	1	2
7	SELECT NUM|'||IDX_OR_TAB||':'||PTYPE||':'||SUBPTYPE||':'||PCNT||':'||SUBPCNT ▦	2	1	2
8	SELECT /*+ full(o) */ U.NAME, COUNT(DECODE(O.TYPE#, 7,1, 8,1, 9,1, 11,1, ▦	1	1	1
9	delete from WRH$_SQL_PLAN tab where (:beg_snap <= tab.snap_id and ▦	1	1	1
10	delete from WRH$_BG_EVENT_SUMMARY tab where (:beg_snap <= tab.snap ▦	1	1	1
11	select name,type#,obj#,remoteowner,linkname,namespace, subname from obj$ v ▦	1	1	1
12	select name, type#, obj#, remoteowner, linkname, namespace, subname from ob ▦	1	1	1
13	select name, type#, obj#, remoteowner, linkname, namespace, subname from ob ▦	1	1	1
14	delete from wrh$_sqltext tab where (tab.dbid = :dbid and :beg_snap <= tab. ▦	1	1	1
15	select grantor#,ta.obj#,ta.type# from objauth$ ta, obj$ o where grantee#=:1 and t ▦	1	1	1
16	select name, type#, obj#, remoteowner, linkname, namespace, subname from ob ▦	1	1	1
17	select name, type#, obj#, remoteowner, linkname, namespace, subname from ob ▦	1	1	1
18	delete from WRH$_WAITCLASSMETRIC_HISTORY tab where (:beg_snap <= t ▦	1	1	1
19	delete from WRH$_SYSMETRIC_SUMMARY tab where (:beg_snap <= tab.snap ▦	1	1	1
20	delete from WRH$_ENQUEUE_STAT tab where (:beg_snap <= tab.snap_id and ▦	1	1	1
21	delete from WRI$_ALERT_HISTORY where time_suggested < :1 ▦	1	1	1
22	select max(bytes) from dba_segments ▦	1	1	1

Once the DBA has been assured that the large-table full-table scans are legitimate, those times when they are executed must be known so that a selective parallel query can be implemented, depending on the existing CPU consumption on the server since OPQ drives up CPU consumption and should be invoked when the server can handle the additional load.

🖫 awr_full_table_scans.sql

```
-- **************************************************
-- Copyright © 2005 by Rampant TechPress
-- This script is free for non-commercial purposes
-- with no warranties.  Use at your own risk.
--
-- To license this script for a commercial purpose,
-- contact info@rampant.cc
-- **************************************************

ttile 'Large Full-table scans|Per Snapshot Period'

col c1 heading 'Begin|Interval|time'  format a20
col c4 heading 'FTS|Count'            format 999,999

break on c1 skip 2
break on c2 skip 2

select
  to_char(sn.begin_interval_time,'yy-mm-dd hh24')  c1,
  count(1)                                         c4
from
  dba_hist_sql_plan p,
```

```
   dba_hist_sqlstat   s,
   dba_hist_snapshot sn,
   dba_segments       o
where
   p.object_owner <> 'SYS'
and
   p.object_owner = o.owner
and
   p.object_name = o.segment_name
and
   o.blocks > 1000
and
   p.operation like '%TABLE ACCESS%'
and
   p.options like '%FULL%'
and
   p.sql_id = s.sql_id
and
   s.snap_id = sn.snap_id
group by
  to_char(sn.begin_interval_time,'yy-mm-dd hh24')
order by
  1;
```

The following is the output where overall total counts are seen for full-tables experiencing large-table full-table scans because the scans may be due to a missing index.

```
        Large Full-table scans
         Per Snapshot Period

Begin
Interval                    FTS
time                        Count
-------------------- --------
04-10-18 11                   4
04-10-21 17                   1
04-10-21 23                   2
04-10-22 15                   2
04-10-22 16                   2
04-10-22 23                   2
04-10-24 00                   2
04-10-25 00                   2
04-10-25 10                   2
04-10-25 17                   9
04-10-25 18                   1
04-10-25 21                   1
04-10-26 12                   1
04-10-26 13                   3
04-10-26 14                   3
04-10-26 15                  11
04-10-26 16                   4
04-10-26 17                   4
```

```
04-10-26 18                    3
04-10-26 23                    2
04-10-27 13                    2
04-10-27 14                    3
04-10-27 15                    4
04-10-27 16                    4
04-10-27 17                    3
04-10-27 18                   17
04-10-27 19                    1
04-10-28 12                   22
04-10-28 13                    2
04-10-29 13                    9
```

This data can easily be plotted and any trends for the database can be identified as shown in Figure 10.1.

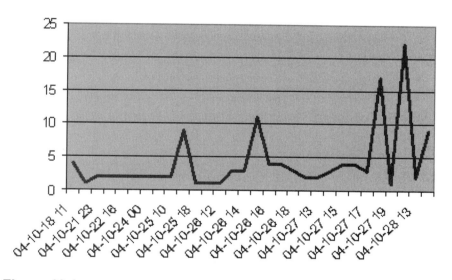

Figure 10.1: *Trends of large-table full-table scans.*

One important use for the AWR and STATSPACK tables is the ability to track table join methods over time. This is especially important for ensuring that the schema queries are using the fastest table join method. The following query produces a table join exception report.

The choice between a hash join, star transformation join, and a nested loop join depends on several factors:

- The relative number of rows in each table.

- The presence of indexes on the key values.

- The settings for static parameters such as *optimizer_index_caching* and *cpu_cost*.

- The current setting and available memory in *pga_aggregate_target*

Hash joins do not use indexes, but they perform multi-block reads, often using a parallel query. Hence, hash joins with parallel full-table scans tend to drive up CPU consumption. Also, PGA memory consumption becomes higher when hash joins are used, but if AMM is enabled, it's not usually a problem.

The following query produces a report alerting an Oracle DBA when a hash join operation count exceeds some set threshold:

🖫 **hash_join_awr.sql**

```
-- ***************************************************
-- Copyright © 2005 by Rampant TechPress
-- This script is free for non-commercial purposes
-- with no warranties.  Use at your own risk.
--
-- To license this script for a commercial purpose,
-- contact info@rampant.cc
-- ***************************************************

col c1 heading 'Date'            format a20
col c2 heading 'Hash|Join|Count'  format 99,999,999
col c3 heading 'Rows|Processed'   format 99,999,999
col c4 heading 'Disk|Reads'       format 99,999,999
col c5 heading 'CPU|Time'         format 99,999,999


accept hash_thr char prompt 'Enter Hash Join Threshold: '

ttitle 'Hash Join Threshold|&hash_thr'
```

```
select
   to_char(sn.begin_interval_time,'yy-mm-dd hh24')  c1,
   count(*)                                         c2,
   sum(st.rows_processed_delta)                     c3,
   sum(st.disk_reads_delta)                         c4,
   sum(st.cpu_time_delta)                           c5
from
   dba_hist_snapshot sn,
   dba_hist_sql_plan  p,
   dba_hist_sqlstat   st
where
   st.sql_id = p.sql_id
and
   sn.snap_id = st.snap_id
and
   p.operation = 'HASH JOIN'
having
   count(*) > &hash_thr
group by
   begin_interval_time;
```

The sample output might look like the following, showing the number of hash joins during the snapshot period along with the relative I/O and CPU associated with the processing. The values for *rows_processed* are generally higher for hash joins, which do full-table scans, as opposed to nested-loop joins, which generally involve a very small set of returned rows.

	Hash Join Thresholds			
Date	Hash Join Count	Rows Processed	Disk Reads	CPU Time
04-10-12 17	22	4,646	887	39,990,515
04-10-13 16	25	2,128	827	54,746,653
04-10-14 11	21	17,368	3,049	77,297,578
04-10-21 15	60	2,805	3,299	5,041,064
04-10-22 10	25	6,864	941	4,077,524
04-10-22 13	31	11,261	2,950	46,207,733
04-10-25 16	35	46,269	1,504	6,364,414

The previous script can be easily modified to track star transformation joins.

Interrogating SQL Execution Plans

The script below examines the execution plans of *plan9i.sql* and reports on the frequency of every type of table and index access including full-table scans, index range scans, index unique scans and index full scans.

plan9i.sql and *plan10g.sql* scripts go to the appropriate view (*v$sql_plan* in *plan9i.sql* and *dba_hist_sqlplan* in *plan10g.sql*) and parse the output, counting the frequency of execution for each type of access. Both scripts were listed earlier in the book and are available in the Code Depot. The *plan9i.sql* script shows the SQL that is currently inside the library cache.

The next section of code is the AWR version of the SQL execution plan script. Unlike the *plan9i.sql* script that only extracts current SQL from the library cache, the *plan10g.sql* script accesses the AWR *dba_hist_sqlplan* table and gives a time-series view of the ways that Oracle is accessing tables and indexes.

The output is shown below. The starting point is a look at the counts of full-table scans (table access full) for each AWR snapshot period. This report gives all the information needed to select candidate tables for the KEEP pool. The database will benefit from placing small tables, less than two percent of *db_cache_size*, that are subject to frequent full-table scans in the KEEP pool. The report from an Oracle Applications database below shows full-table scans on both large and small tables.

The RECYCLE pool should be used for segregating large-tables involved in frequent full-table scans. To locate these large-table full-table scans, one can return to the *plan9i.sql* full-table scan report:

```
                    full table scans and counts

Snapshot Time  OWNER       NAME                      NUM_ROWS C K  BLOCKS  NBR_FTS
-------------  ----------  ------------------------  -------- - -  ------  --------  -----
12/08/04 14    APPLSYS     FND_CONC_RELEASE_DISJS         39 N K       2   98,864
               APPLSYS     FND_CONC_RELEASE_PERIODS       39 N K       2   98,864
               APPLSYS     FND_CONC_RELEASE_STATES         1 N K       2   98,864
               SYS         DUAL                              N K       2   63,466
               APPLSYS     FND_CONC_PP_ACTIONS         7,021 N      1,262   52,036
               APPLSYS     FND_CONC_REL_CONJ_MEMBER        0 N K      22   50,174

12/08/04 15    APPLSYS     FND_CONC_RELEASE_DISJS         39 N K       2   33,811
               APPLSYS     FND_CONC_RELEASE_PERIODS       39 N K       2    2,864
               APPLSYS     FND_CONC_RELEASE_STATES         1 N K       2   32,864
               SYS         DUAL                              N K       2   63,466
               APPLSYS     FND_CONC_PP_ACTIONS         7,021 N      1,262   12,033
               APPLSYS     FND_CONC_REL_CONJ_MEMBER        0 N K      22   50,174
```

One table in the listing is a clear candidate for inclusion in the RECYCLE pool. The *fnd_conc_pp_actions* table contains 1,262 blocks and has experienced many full-table scans.

Examining this report, three files can be quickly identified that should be moved to the KEEP pool by selecting the tables with less than 50 blocks that have no "K" designation.

Oracle developed the KEEP pool to fully cache blocks from frequently accessed tables and indexes in a separate buffer.

When determining the size of the KEEP pool, the number of bytes comprising all tables that will reside in the KEEP area must be totaled. This will insure that the KEEP buffer is large enough to fully cache all the tables that have been assigned to it.

These scripts also show counts for indexes that are accessed via rowid, indicative of non-range scan access.

```
Table access by ROWID and counts
Wed Dec 22


Snapshot Time  OWNER    NAME                     NUM_ROWS  NBR_RID
-------------  -------  -----------------------  --------  --------
12/16/04 19    SYSMAN   MGMT_TARGET_ROLLUP_TIMES      110       10
12/17/04 06    SYSMAN   MGMT_TARGET_ROLLUP_TIMES      110       10
12/17/04 07    SYSMAN   MGMT_TARGET_ROLLUP_TIMES      110       10
12/17/04 08    SYSMAN   MGMT_TARGET_ROLLUP_TIMES      110       10
12/17/04 12    SYSMAN   MGMT_TARGET_ROLLUP_TIMES      110       10
12/17/04 13    SYSMAN   MGMT_TARGET_ROLLUP_TIMES      110       10
12/17/04 14    SYS      VIEW$                       2,583       84
               SYSMAN   MGMT_TARGET_ROLLUP_TIMES      110       10
12/17/04 17    SYS      VIEW$                       2,583       82
12/17/04 18    SYSMAN   MGMT_TARGET_ROLLUP_TIMES      110       10
```

```
12/17/04 20    SYSMAN    MGMT_TARGET_ROLLUP_TIMES        110    10
12/17/04 21    SYSMAN    MGMT_TARGET_ROLLUP_TIMES        110    10
12/17/04 22    SYSMAN    MGMT_TARGET_ROLLUP_TIMES        110    10
12/17/04 23    SYSMAN    MGMT_TARGET_ROLLUP_TIMES        110    10
12/18/04 00    SYSMAN    MGMT_TARGET_ROLLUP_TIMES        110    10
12/18/04 01    SYSMAN    MGMT_TARGET_ROLLUP_TIMES        110    20
12/18/04 02    SYSMAN    MGMT_TARGET_ROLLUP_TIMES        110    10
12/18/04 03    SYSMAN    MGMT_TARGET_ROLLUP_TIMES        110    10
12/18/04 04    SYSMAN    MGMT_TARGET_ROLLUP_TIMES        110    10
12/18/04 05    SYSMAN    MGMT_TARGET_ROLLUP_TIMES        110    10
12/18/04 09    SYSMAN    MGMT_TARGET_ROLLUP_TIMES        110    20
12/18/04 11    SYSMAN    MGMT_TARGET_ROLLUP_TIMES        110    20
```

It also yields counts of index full scans and index range scans, and this data is very useful for locating those indexes that might benefit from segregation onto a larger blocksize.

```
Index full scans and counts

Snapshot Time   OWNER      TABLE_NAME              INDEX_NAME           TBL_BLOCKS  NBR_SCANS
--------------- ---------- ----------------------  -------------------- ----------  ---------
12/08/04 14     SYSMAN     MGMT_FAILOVER_TABLE     PK_MGMT_FAILOVER              8         59
12/08/04 15     SYSMAN     MGMT_FAILOVER_TABLE     PK_MGMT_FAILOVER              8         58
12/08/04 16     SYS        WRH$_TEMPFILE           WRH$_TEMPFILE_PK             8         16
                SYSMAN     MGMT_FAILOVER_TABLE     PK_MGMT_FAILOVER              8         59
12/08/04 17     SYS        WRH$_STAT_NAME          WRH$_STAT_NAME_P             8        483
                SYSMAN     MGMT_FAILOVER_TABLE     PK_MGMT_FAILOVER              8         58
12/08/04 18     SYSMAN     MGMT_FAILOVER_TABLE     PK_MGMT_FAILOVER              8         59
12/08/04 19     SYSMAN     MGMT_FAILOVER_TABLE     PK_MGMT_FAILOVER              8         58
12/08/04 20     SYSMAN     MGMT_FAILOVER_TABLE     PK_MGMT_FAILOVER              8         59
12/08/04 21     SYSMAN     MGMT_FAILOVER_TABLE     PK_MGMT_FAILOVER              8         58
12/08/04 22     SYSMAN     MGMT_FAILOVER_TABLE     PK_MGMT_FAILOVER              8         58
12/08/04 23     SYSMAN     MGMT_FAILOVER_TABLE     PK_MGMT_FAILOVER              8         59
12/09/04 00     SYSMAN     MGMT_FAILOVER_TABLE     PK_MGMT_FAILOVER              8         58
12/09/04 01     SYSMAN     MGMT_FAILOVER_TABLE     PK_MGMT_FAILOVER              8         59
12/09/04 02     SYSMAN     MGMT_FAILOVER_TABLE     PK_MGMT_FAILOVER              8         59
12/09/04 03     SYSMAN     MGMT_FAILOVER_TABLE     PK_MGMT_FAILOVER              8         59
12/09/04 04     SYSMAN     MGMT_FAILOVER_TABLE     PK_MGMT_FAILOVER              8         58
12/09/04 05     SYSMAN     MGMT_FAILOVER_TABLE     PK_MGMT_FAILOVER              8         59
12/09/04 06     SYSMAN     MGMT_FAILOVER_TABLE     PK_MGMT_FAILOVER              8         58
12/09/04 07     SYSMAN     MGMT_FAILOVER_TABLE     PK_MGMT_FAILOVER              8         59
12/09/04 08     SYSMAN     MGMT_FAILOVER_TABLE     PK_MGMT_FAILOVER              8         58
12/09/04 09     SYSMAN     MGMT_FAILOVER_TABLE     PK_MGMT_FAILOVER              8         59
```

```
Index range scans and counts

Snapshot Time OWNER    TABLE_NAME              INDEX_NAME               TBL_BLOCKS  NBR_SCANS
------------- -------  ----------------------  ------------------------ ----------  ---------
12/08/04 14   SYS      SYSAUTH$                I_SYSAUTH1                        8        345
              SYSMAN   MGMT_JOB_EXECUTION      MGMT_JOB_EXEC_IDX01               8       1373
              SYSMAN   MGMT_JOB_EXEC_SUMMARY   MGMT_JOB_EXEC_SUMM_IDX04          8         59
              SYSMAN   MGMT_METRICS            MGMT_METRICS_IDX_01              80         59
              SYSMAN   MGMT_PARAMETERS         MGMT_PARAMETERS_IDX_01            8        179
              SYSMAN   MGMT_TARGETS            MGMT_TARGETS_IDX_02               8         61
12/08/04 15   SYS      SYSAUTH$                I_SYSAUTH1                        8        273
              SYSMAN   MGMT_JOB_EXECUTION      MGMT_JOB_EXEC_IDX01               8       1423
              SYSMAN   MGMT_JOB_EXEC_SUMMARY   MGMT_JOB_EXEC_SUMM_IDX04          8         58
```

Now that information on SQL monitoring has been presented, the next section will provide details on how the DBA can improve SQL execution with statistics collection and manipulation.

Statistics for the Oracle SQL Optimizer

The choices of executions plans made by the CBO are only as good as the statistics available to it. The old-fashioned analyze table and *dbms_utility* methods for generating CBO statistics are obsolete and somewhat dangerous to SQL performance since the CBO uses object statistics to choose the best execution plan for all SQL statements.

The better the quality of the statistics, the better the job that the CBO will do when determining execution plans. Unfortunately, doing a complete analysis on a large database could take days, and most shops must sample the database to get CBO statistics. The goal is to take a large enough sample of the database to provide top quality data for the CBO and choose the best parameters for the *dbms_stats* utility.

In Oracle10g, statistics collections are automated, but DBAs may still need to selectively add histograms and other specialized optimizer statistics. By setting the most appropriate baseline values for static initialization parameters, a huge amount of work can be saved when detailed SQL tuning is undertaken. A quick look at object tuning follows in the next section.

Managing Schema Statistics with *dbms_stats*

Experts agree that most of the common SQL problems can be avoided if statistics are carefully defined and managed. In order for the CBO to make an intelligent decision about the best execution plan for the SQL, the CBO must have information about the table and indexes that participate in the query. This information includes:

- The size of the tables.

- The indexes on the tables.

- The distribution of column values.

- The cardinality of intermediate result sets.

- The selectivity of column values.

Given this information, the CBO can make an informed analysis and almost always generates the best execution plan. The following section presents areas of CBO statistics that will be examined so that the DBA can gather top quality statistics for the CBO and create an appropriate CBO environment for their database.

Getting Top-Quality Statistics with *dbms_stats*

Many experts believe that the execution plan selected is only as good as the optimizer statistics available to the query. The old fashioned analyze table and *dbms_utility* methods for collecting schema statistics are obsolete and somewhat dangerous to SQL performance. The CBO uses object statistics to choose the best execution plan for all SQL statements.

The *dbms_stats* utility does a far better job in estimating statistics, especially for large partitioned tables, and the better statistics result in faster SQL execution plans. The following is a sample execution of dbms_stats with the options clause:

```
exec dbms_stats.gather_schema_stats( -
   ownname          => 'SCOTT', -
   options          => 'GATHER AUTO', -
   estimate_percent => dbms_stats.auto_sample_size, -
   method_opt       => 'for all columns size repeat', -
   degree           => 34 -
   )
```

There are several values for the options parameter that are important to know:

- **gather** - This option re-analyzes the whole schema.

- **gather empty** - This option only analyzes objects that have no statistics.

- **gather stale** - This option is used with the monitoring feature and only re-analyzes tables with more than 10 percent modifications (inserts, updates, deletes).

- **gather auto** - This option will re-analyze objects that currently have no statistics and objects with stale statistics. Using the gather auto option is like combining gather stale and gather empty options.

Both the gather stale and gather auto *dbms_stats* option require monitoring. Table monitoring can be implemented with the alter table xxx monitoring command, and once issued, Oracle tracks changed tables with the *dba_tab_modifications* view. The *dba_tab_modifications* table contains the cumulative number of inserts, updates and deletes tracked since the last analysis of statistics.

The most interesting of the *dbms_stats* options is the gather stale option. All statistics will become stale quickly in a robust OLTP database, so DBA's must remember the rule for gather stale is > 10% row change based on *num_rows* at statistics collection time.

Hence, almost every table except read-only tables will be reanalyzed with the gather stale option, making the gather stale option best for systems that are largely read-only. For example, if only five percent of the database tables get significant updates, then only five percent of the tables will be reanalyzed with the gather stale option.

To aid in intelligent histogram generation, Oracle uses the *method_opt* parameter of *dbms_stats*. There are also important new options within the method_opt clause, namely skewonly, repeat and auto:

```
method_opt=>'for all columns size skewonly'

method_opt=>'for all columns size repeat'

method_opt=>'for all columns size auto'
```

The *skewonly* option is very time intensive because it examines the distribution of values for every column within every index.

If *dbms_stats* finds an index whose columns are unevenly distributed, it will create a histogram for that index to aid the cost-based SQL optimizer in making a decision about index versus full-table scan access. For example, if an index has one column that is in 50 percent of the rows, a full-table scan is faster than an index scan to retrieve these rows.

```
--*************************************************************
-- SKEWONLY option-Detailed analysis
--
-- Use this method for a first-time analysis for skewed indexes
-- This runs a long time because all indexes are examined
--*************************************************************
begin
  dbms_stats.gather_schema_stats(
     ownname          => 'SCOTT',
     estimate_percent => dbms_stats.auto_sample_size,
     method_opt       => 'for all columns size skewonly',
      degree          => 7
   );
end;
```

If statistics need to be reanalyzed, the task will be less resource intensive with the repeat option. Using the repeat option, Oracle will only reanalyze indexes with existing histograms and will not search for other histograms opportunities. This is the way that statistics should be reanalyzed on a regular basis.

```
--*************************************************************
-- REPEAT OPTION - Only reanalyze histograms for indexes
-- that have histograms
--
-- Following the initial analysis, the weekly analysis
-- job will use the "repeat" option. The repeat option
-- tells dbms_stats that no indexes have changed, and
-- it will only reanalyze histograms for
```

```
-- indexes that have histograms.
--******************************************************
begin
   dbms_stats.gather_schema_stats(
      ownname          => 'SCOTT',
      estimate_percent => dbms_stats.auto_sample_size,
      method_opt       => 'for all columns size repeat',
      degree           => 7
   );
end;
```

The AUTO option within *dbms_stats* is used when Oracle table monitoring is implemented using the "alter table xxx" monitoring; command. The auto option will create histograms based upon data distribution and the manner in which the column is accessed by the application as determined by the volume of updates to the table. Using *method_opt=>*'auto' is very similar to using the gather auto in the option parameter of *dbms_stats*.

```
begin
  dbms_stats.gather_schema_stats(
     ownname          => 'SCOTT',
      estimate_percent => dbms_stats.auto_sample_size,
      method_opt       => 'for all columns size auto',
      degree           => 7
   );
end;
```

dbms_stats can be made to analyze schema statistics very quickly on SMP servers with multiple CPU's. Oracle allows for parallelism when collecting CBO statistics, which can greatly speed up the time required to collect statistics. A parallel statistics collection requires an SMP server with multiple CPUs.

The following section will examine the importance of estimating the optimal sample size when gathering schema statistics.

Automating Statistics Sample Size with *dbms_stats*

The higher the quality of the schema statistics, the higher the probability that CBO will choose the optimal execution plan.

Unfortunately, doing a complete analysis of every row of every table in the schema could take days and most shops must sample their database to get CBO statistics.

The goal of estimating the sample size is to take a large enough sample of the database to provide top quality data for the CBO while not adversely impacting server resources. Now that information has been presented on how the *dbms_stats* option works, it is time to examine how to specify an adequate sample size for *dbms_stats*.

In earlier releases, the DBA had to guess what percentage of the database provided the best sample size. This could cause the schema to be underanalyzed. Starting with Oracle9i Database, the *estimate_percent* argument was added to *dbms_stats* to allow Oracle to automatically estimate the best percentage of a segment to sample when gathering statistics. The following is a sample invocation:

```
estimate_percent => dbms_stats.auto_sample_size
```

After collecting statistics with an automatic sample size, the accuracy of the automatic statistics sampling can be verified by looking at the SAMPLE_SIZE column on any of the DBA data dictionary object views.

In practice, the *auto_sample_size* option of *dbms_stats* generally chooses a *sample_size* from 5 to 20 percent when using automatic sampling, depending on the size of the tables and the distribution of column values.

The selection of a sample that is too small can impact the CBO and it is the DBA's responsibility to ensure that there is a statistically significant sample size for every object in their schema. The following section presents some methods DBA's use to ensure that their SQL optimizer always has great schema statistics.

Statistics Management for the DBA

Many infrastructure issues must be addressed in order to avoid surprises with SQL optimization. Shops that do not create this infrastructure are plagued by constantly changing SQL execution plans and poor database performance.

All Oracle DBA's should carefully manage the CBO statistics to ensure that the CBO works the same in their test and production environments. A savvy DBA knows how to collect high quality statistics and migrate production statistics into the test environments. This approach ensures that all SQL migrating into production has the same execution plan as it did in the test database.

It is very rare for the fundamental nature of a schema to change; large tables remain large, and index columns rarely change distribution, cardinality, or skew. It is only necessary to consider periodically re-analyzing the total schema statistics if the database matches the following criteria:

- **CPU-Intensive Databases** - Many scientific systems load a small set of experimental data, analyze the data, produce reports, and then truncate and reload a new set of experiments. For these types of systems it may be necessary to reanalyze the schema each time the database is reloaded.

- **Highly Volatile Databases** - In these rare cases, the size of table and the characteristics of index column data changes radically. For example, if a table has 100 rows one week and 10,000 rows the next week, a periodic reanalysis of statistics might be prudent.

The key to success with the CBO is stability and ensuring success with the CBO involves several important infrastructure issues.

Ensure Static Execution Plans

Whenever an object is reanalyzed, the execution plan for thousands of SQL statements can be changed. Most successful Oracle sites will choose to lock down their SQL execution plans by carefully controlling CBO statistics, using stored outlines (optimizer plan stability), adding detailed hints to their SQL, or by using Oracle10g SQL Profiles.

Reanalyze CBO Statistics only When Necessary

One of the most common mistakes made by Oracle DBA's is to frequently reanalyze the schema. The sole purpose of reanalysis is to change the execution plans for the SQL, and if it's not broken, don't fix it. If current SQL performance is satisfactory, reanalyzing a schema could cause significant performance problems and undo the tuning efforts of the development staff. In practice, very few shops are sufficiently dynamic to require periodic schema reanalysis.

Pre-Tune the SQL before Deploying

Many Oracle systems developers assume that their sole goal is to write SQL statements that deliver the correct data from Oracle. In reality, writing the SQL is only half their job. Successful Oracle sites require all developers to ensure that their SQL accesses Oracle in an optimal fashion.

Savvy Oracle developers know the most efficient way to code Oracle SQL for optimal execution plans, and savvy Oracle shops train their developers to formulate efficient SQL.

DBA's and their staff should train themselves to use the autotrace and TKPROF utilities and to interpret SQL execution results. Prior to Oracle10g, it was an important job of the Oracle DBA to properly gather and distribute statistics for the CBO. The goal of the DBA was to keep the most accurate production statistics for the current processing. In some cases, there may be more than one set of optimal statistics.

For example, the best statistics for OLTP processing may not be the best statistics for the data warehouse processing that occurs each evening. In this case, the DBA will keep two sets of statistics and import them into the schema when processing modes change.

The following section presents information on how Oracle SQL optimization can be adjusted by adding histograms.

Tuning SQL with Histograms

The distribution of values within an index will often affect the CBO's decision whether to perform a full-table scan to satisfy a query or to use an index. This can happen whenever the column referenced within a SQL query WHERE clause has a non-uniform distribution of values, making a full-table scan cheaper than index access.

Only when there are highly skewed values in a column should histograms be created. While this rarely happens, a common mistake a DBA can make is the unnecessary collection of histograms in the statistics. The CBO will use the literal value in the query's WHERE clause and will compare it to the histogram statistics bucket when a column's values are not distributed evenly.

Histograms are used to predict cardinality and the number of rows returned to a query. Assume that there is a *vehicle_type* index and that 65 percent of the values are for the CAR type. Whenever a query with where *vehicle_type* = 'CAR' is specified, a full-table scan would be the fastest execution plan, while a query with where *vehicle_type* = 'TRUCK' would be faster when using access via an index.

Since they affect performance, histograms should only be used when they are required for a faster CBO execution plan. Histograms incur additional overhead during the parsing phase of an SQL query and can be used effectively only when:

- A column's values cause the CBO to make an incorrect guess - If the CBO makes a wrong assumption about the size of an intermediate result set, it may choose a sub-optimal execution plan. A histogram added to the column often provides the additional information required for the CBO to choose the best plan.

- Significant skewing exists in the distribution of a column's data values - The skew must be important enough to make the CBO choose another execution plan.

- A table column is referenced in one or more queries - Never create histograms if queries do not reference the column. Novice DBAs may mistakenly create histograms on a skewed column, even if it is not referenced in a query.

Each DBA will likely have an opinion on this, but regardless, such a query can assist in identifying SQL statements that have the potential to cause system slowdowns. The following section provides information on another exciting new SQL optimization feature, Dynamic Sampling.

Oracle10g Dynamic Sampling

One of the greatest problems with the Oracle CBO was the failure of the Oracle DBA to gather accurate schema statistics. Even with the *dbms_stats* package, the schema statistics were often stale and the DBA did not always create histograms for skewed data columns and data columns that are used to estimate the size of SQL intermediate result sets.

This resulted in a bum rap for Oracle's CBO, and beginner DBA's often falsely accused the CBO of failing to generate optimal execution plans when the real cause of the sub-optimal execution plan was the DBA's failure to collect complete schema statistics.

Using the enhanced *dbms_stats* package, Oracle will automatically estimate the sample size, detect skewed columns that would benefit from histograms, and refresh the schema statistics when they become stale. This automates a very important DBA task and ensures that Oracle always has the statistics that it needs to make good execution plan choices.

However, there was always a nagging problem with the CBO. Even with good statistics, the CBO would sometimes determine a sub-optimal table-join order causing unnecessarily large intermediate result sets.

Even with the best schema statistics, it can be impossible to predict the optimal table join order, the table join order that has the smallest intermediate baggage. As can be expected, reducing the size of the intermediate row sets can greatly improve the speed of the query.

If one were to assume that there is a three-way table join against tables that all contain over 10,000 rows each. This database has

50,000 student rows, 10,000 course rows and 5,000 professor rows as shown in Figure 10.2.

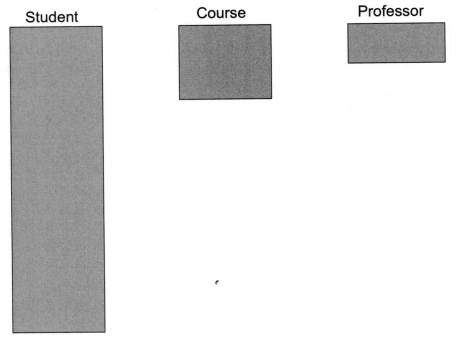

Figure 10.2: *Number of rows in each table.*

If the number of rows in the table determined the best table join order, the expectation would be that any 3-way table join would start by joining the professor and course tables, and then join the RESULT set to the student table.

However, whenever there is a WHERE clause, the total number of rows in each table does not matter if index access is being used. The following is the query:

```
select
   student_name
from
   professor
natural join
   course
natural join
   student
where
   professor = 'jones'
and
   course = 'anthropology 610';

Stan Nowakowski
Bob Crane
James Bakke
Patty O'Furniture

4 Rows selected.
```

Despite the huge numbers of rows in each table, the final result set will only be four rows. If the CBO can predict the size of the final result, sampling techniques can be used to examine the WHERE clause of the query and determine which two tables should be joined first.

There are only two table join choices in this simplified example:

- Join (student to course) and (RESULT to professor).

- Join (professor to course) and (RESULT to student).

Which option is better? The best solution will be the one where RESULT is smallest. Since the query is filtered with a WHERE clause, the number of rows in each table is incidental, and the real concern is about the number of rows where professor = 'jones' and where course = 'Anthropology 610'.

If this information is already known, the best table join order becomes obvious. Assume that Professor Jones is very popular and teaches 50 courses and that Anthropology 610 has a total of eight students. Knowing this, it becomes apparent that the size of the intermediate row baggage is very different if the intial join is (professor to course) followed by (RESULT to student). This is shown in Figure 10.3:

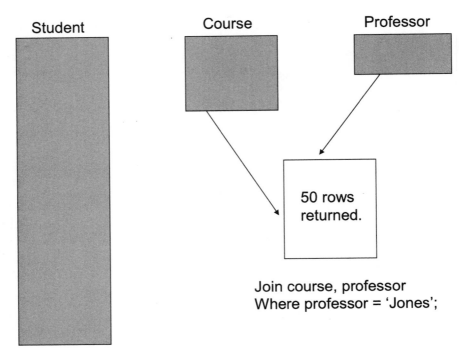

Figure 10.3: *A sub-optimal intermediate row size.*

If the CBO were to join the student table to the course table first, the intermediate result set would only be eight rows, far less baggage to carry over to the final join if the join order is (student to course) and (RESULT to professor).

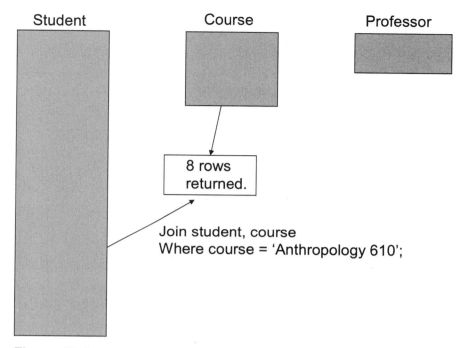

Figure 10.4: *An optimal intermediate row size.*

Now that there are only eight rows returned from the first query, it easy to join the tiny 8-row result set into the professor table to get the final answer.

How is Join Cardinality Estimated?

In the absence of column histograms, the Oracle CBO must be able to guess on this information. Sometimes the guesses are wrong. This is one reason why the ORDERED hint is one of the most popular SQL tuning hints. Use of the ORDERED hint allows the DBA to specify that the tables be joined together in the same order that they appear in the FROM clause, like this:

```
select /+ ORDERED */
   student_name
from
   student
natural join
   course
natural join
   professor
where
   professor = 'jones'
and
   course = 'anthropology 610';
```

If the values for the professor and course table columns are not skewed, it is unlikely that the 10g automatic statistics would have created histograms buckets in the *dba_histograms* view for these columns.

The Oracle CBO needs to be able to accurately estimate the final number of rows returned by each step of the query. The schema metadata from running *dbms_stats* is then used to choose the table join order that results in the least amount of baggage (intermediate rows) from each of the table join operations. This can be a daunting task. When an SQL query has a complex WHERE clause it can be very difficult to estimate the size of the intermediate result sets, especially when the WHERE clause transforms column values with mathematical functions.

Oracle9i introduced the new dynamic sampling method for gathering run-time schema statistics, and it is now enabled by default in Oracle10g. However, dynamic sampling is not for every database. When *dynamic_sampling* was first introduced in Oracle9i, it was used primarily for data warehouse system with complex queries. Since it is enabled by default in Oracle10g, the DBA may want to turn off *dynamic_sampling* to remove unnecessary overhead if any of the following are true:

- The application is an online transaction processing (OLTP) database with small, single-table queries.

- The database queries are not frequently re-executed, as determined by the EXECUTIONS column in *v$sql* and *executions_delta* in *dba_hist_sqlstat*.

- The system's multi-table joins have simple WHERE clause predicates with single-column values and no built-in or mathematical functions.

Dynamic sampling is ideal whenever a query is going to execute multiple times because the sample time is small compared to the overall query execution time. By sampling data from the table at runtime, Oracle10g can quickly evaluate complex WHERE clause predicates and determine the selectivity of each predicate, using this information to determine the optimal table join order.

Sample Table Scans

A sample table scan retrieves a random sample of data of whatever size is chosen. The sample can be from a simple table or a complex SELECT statement such as a statement involving multiple joins and complex views.

Some simple SQL queries can be run to peek inside dynamic sampling. The following SQL statement uses a sample block and sample rows scan on the customer table. There are 50,000 rows in this table. The first statement shows a sample block scan and the last SQL statement shows a sample row scan.

```
select
   count(*)
from
   customer
   sample block(20);


   COUNT(*)
----------
    12268
```

```
select
   pol_no,
   sales_id,
   sum_assured,
   premium
from
   customer
   sample (0.02) ;
```

```
    POL_NO    SALES_ID SUM_ASSURED    PREMIUM
---------- ---------- ----------- ---------- --
      2895         10        2525          2
      3176         10        2525          2
      9228         10        2525          2
     11294         11        2535          4
     19846         11        2535          4
     25547         12        2545          6
     29583         12        2545          6
     40042         13        2555          8
     47331         14        2565         10
     45283         14        2565         10
```

10 rows selected.

Just as the data can be sampled with SQL, the Oracle10g CBO can sample the data prior to formulating the execution plan. For example, the new *dynamic_sampling* SQL hint can be used to sample rows from the table:

```
select /*+ dynamic_sampling (customer 10) */
   pol_no,
   sales_id,
   sum_assured,
   premium
from
   customer;
```

```
    POL_NO    SALES_ID SUM_ASSURED    PREMIUM
---------- ---------- ----------- ---------- --
      2895         10        2525          2
      3176         10        2525          2
      9228         10        2525          2
     11294         11        2535          4
     19846         11        2535          4
     25547         12        2545          6
     29583         12        2545          6
     40042         13        2555          8
     47331         14        2565         10
     45283         14        2565         10
```

10 rows selected.

Dynamic sampling addresses an innate problem in SQL and this issue is common to all relational databases. Estimating the optimal join order involves guessing the sequence that results in the smallest amount of intermediate row sets, and it is impossible to collect every possible combination of WHERE clauses without real experience upon which to base statistics.

Dynamic sampling is a godsend for databases that have large n-way table joins that execute frequently. By sampling a tiny subset of the data, the Oracle 10g CBO gleans clues as to the fastest table join order.

dynamic_sampling does not take a long time to execute, but it can be an unnecessary overhead for all Oracle10g databases. Dynamic sampling is just another example of Oracle's commitment to making Oracle10g an intelligent, self-optimizing database.

This section presented detailed information on the role of schema statistics and dynamic sampling in optimal SQL execution. The next step involves information about SQL tuning with temporary tables.

SQL Tuning with Temporary Tables

It is well understood that Oracle SQL can run faster when complex subqueries are replaced with global temporary tables. Starting in Oracle9i release 2, there was an incorporation of a subquery factoring utility which implemented the SQL-99 WITH clause. The WITH clause is a tool for materializing subqueries to save Oracle from having to recompute them multiple times.

The SQL WITH clause is very similar to the use of Global temporary tables (GTT), a technique that is often used to improve query speed for complex subqueries. The following are some important notes about the Oracle WITH clause:

- The SQL WITH clause only works on Oracle 9i release 2 and later.

- Formally, the WITH clause is called subquery factoring.

- The SQL WITH clause is used when a subquery is executed multiple times.

- The ANSI WITH clause is also useful for recursive queries, but this feature has not yet been implemented in Oracle SQL.

The following section will provide information on how the Oracle SQL WITH clause works and see how the WITH clause and Global temporary tables can be used to speed up Oracle queries.

All Stores with Above Average Sales

To keep it simple, the following example only references the aggregations once, where the SQL WITH clause is normally used when an aggregation is referenced multiple times in a query.

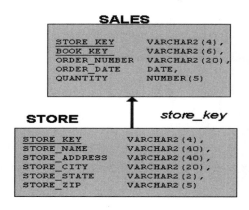

Here is an example of a request to see the names of all stores with above average sales. For each store, average sales must be compared to the average sales for all stores.

Essentially, the query below accesses the STORE and SALES tables, comparing the sales for each store with the average sales for all stores. To answer this query, the following must be known:

- The total sales for all stores.

- The number of stores.

- The sum of sales for each store.

To answer this in a single SQL statement, in-line views as well as a subquery inside a HAVING clause will have to be employed:

```
select
   store_name,
   sum(quantity)
store_sales,
   (select sum(quantity) from sales)/(select count(*) from store)
avg_sales
from
   store   s,
   sales   sl
where
   s.store_key = sl.store_key
having
   sum(quantity) > (select sum(quantity) from sales)/(select
count(*) from store)
group by
   store_name
;
```

While this query provides the correct answer, it is difficult to read and complex to execute, recomputing the sum of sales multiple times. To prevent the unnecessary re-execution of the aggregation (sum(sales)), temporary tables could be created and uses to simplify the query.

- Create a table t1 to hold the total sales for all stores.

- Create a table t2 to hold the number of stores.

- Create a table t3 to hold the store name and the sum of sales for each store.

Then, write a fourth SQL statement that uses tables t1, t2, and t3 to replicate the output from the original query.

The final answer will look like this:

```
create table t1 as
select sum(quantity) all_sales from stores;

create table t2 as
select count(*) nbr_stores from stores;

create table t3 as
select store_name, sum(quantity) store_sales from store natural join
sales;


select
   store_name
from
   t1,
   t2,
   t3
where
   store_sales > (all_sales / nbr_stores)
;
```

While this is a very elegant and easy to understand solution with a faster execution time, the SQL-99 WITH clause can also be used instead of temporary tables. The Oracle SQL WITH clause will compute the aggregation once, give it a name, and allow it to be referenced, perhaps multiple times, later in the query.

The SQL-99 WITH clause is very confusing at first because the SQL statement does not begin with the word SELECT. Instead, the WITH clause is used to start the SQL query, defining the aggregations, which can then be named in the main query as if they were real tables:

```
WITH
    subquery_name
AS
   (the aggregation SQL statement)
SELECT
   (query naming subquery_name);
```

Retuning to the oversimplified example, the temporary tables can be replaced with the SQL WITH clause:

```
WITH
   sum_sales      AS
      select /*+ materialize */
      sum(quantity) all_sales from stores
   number_stores  AS
      select /*+ materialize */
      count(*) nbr_stores from stores;
   sales_by_store AS
      select /*+ materialize */
      store_name, sum(quantity) store_sales from
      store natural join sales
SELECT
   store_name
FROM
   store,
   sum_sales,
   number_stores,
   sales_by_store
WHERE
   store_sales > (all_sales / nbr_stores)
;
```

This example uses the Oracle undocumented materialize hint in the WITH clause. The Oracle materialize hint is used to ensure that the Oracle CBO materializes the temporary tables that are created inside the WITH clause. This is not necessary in Oracle10g, but it helps ensure that the tables are only created one time.

 **Tip!** Depending on the release of Oracle, the use of global temporary tables (GTT) might be a better solution than the WITH clause because indexes can be created on the GTT for faster performance.

The following are some real world SQL tuning silver bullets.

Use Function-Based Indexes (FBI)

In almost all cases, the use of a built-in function (e.g. *to_char*, *decode*, *substr*, etc.) in an SQL query may cause a full-table scan of the target table. To avoid this problem, many Oracle DBAs will create corresponding indexes that make use of function-based indexes. If a corresponding function-based index matches the built-in function of the query, Oracle will be able to service the query with an index range scan thereby avoiding a potentially expensive full-table scan.

A simple example can be used to illustrate. Suppose a SQL statement with hundreds of full-table scans against a large table is identified using a built-in function (BIF) in the WHERE clause of the query. After examining the SQL, it appears that it is accessing a customer by converting the customer name to uppercase using the upper BIF.

```
select
   c.customer_name,
   o.order_date
from
   customer c,
   order    o
where
  upper(c.customer_name) = upper(:v1)
and
   c.cust_nbr = o.cust_nbr
;
```

Running the explain plan utility confirms suspicions that the upper BIF is responsible for an unnecessary large-table full-table scan.

OPTIONS	OBJECT_NAME	POSITION
SELECT STATEMENT		
NESTED LOOPS		4
TABLE ACCESS		1
FULL	CUSTOMER	1
TABLE ACCESS		
BY INDEX ROWID	ORDER	2
INDEX		
RANGE SCAN	CUST_NBR_IDX	1

The table access full customer option confirms suspicions that this BIF is not using the existing index on the CUSTOMER_NAME column. Since it is known that a matching function-based index may change the execution plan, a function-based index is added on upper(CUSTOMER_NAME).

It is often risky to add indexes to a table because the execution plans of many queries may change. However, this problem does not exist with a function-based index because Oracle will only use this type of index when the query uses a matching BIF.

```
create index
   upper_cust_name_idx
on
   customer
     (upper(customer_name))
  tablespace customer
  pctfree 10
  storage
   (initial 128k next 128k maxextents 2147483645 pctincrease 0);
```

Now the SQL can be re-examined and it will become apparent that the full-table scan has been replaced by an index range scan on the new function-based index. For this query, the execution time has been reduced from 45 seconds to less than two seconds.

```
OPERATION
--------------------------------------------------------------------------------
OPTIONS                          OBJECT_NAME                     POSITION
-------------------------------  ----------------------------   ----------
SELECT STATEMENT
                                                                     5
   NESTED LOOPS
                                                                     1
      TABLE ACCESS
BY INDEX ROWID                   CUSTOMER                            1
         INDEX
RANGE SCAN                       CUST_NBR_IDX                        1
      TABLE ACCESS
BY INDEX ROWID                   ORDER                               2
         INDEX
RANGE SCAN                       UPPER_CUST_NAME_IDX                 1
```

This simple example serves to illustrate the foremost SQL tuning rule for BIFs. Whenever a BIF is used in an SQL statement, a function-based index must be created.

Silver Bullet

Use Temporary Tables

The prudent use of temporary tables can dramatically improve Oracle SQL performance. To illustrate the concept, consider the following example from the DBA world. In the query that follows, the goal is to identify all users who exist within Oracle who have not been granted a role. The query could be formulated as an anti-join with a non-correlated subquery as shown:

```
select
   username
from
   dba_users
where
   username NOT IN
      (select grantee from dba_role_privs);
```

This query runs in 18 seconds. These anti-joins can often be replaced with an outer join, but another option exists with the use of temporary tables. The same query is rewritten to utilize temporary tables by selecting the distinct values from each table.

```
drop table temp1;
drop table temp2;

create table
   temp1
as
  select
      username
    from
      dba_users;

create table
   temp2
as
  select distinct
      grantee
    from
      dba_role_privs;

select
   username
from
   temp1
where
   username not in
      (select grantee from temp2);
```

With the addition of temporary tables to hold the intermediate results, this query runs in less than three seconds, a performance increase of a factor of six. It is not easy to quantify the reason for this speed increase since the DBA views do not map directly to Oracle tables; however, it is clear that temporary table shows promise for improving the execution speed of certain types of Oracle SQL queries.

Fix Missing CBO Statistics

A client that had just moved their system into production was experiencing a serious performance problem. The emergency support DBA found that the *optimizer_mode*=choose and there was only one table with statistics. The DBA was running cost-based but seemed completely unaware of the necessity to analyze the schema for CBO statistics.

The trouble began when the DBA wanted to know the average row length for a table. After using a Google search to determine that the location of that information was the *dba_tables.avg_row_len*, it was determined that the values were null. The DBA then went to MetaLink and learned that an analyze table command would fill in the *avg_row_len* column.

CBO will dynamically estimate statistics for all tables with missing statistics and when using *optimizer_mode*=choose with only one table analyzed, any SQL that touches the table will be optimized as a cost-based query. In this case, a multi-step silver bullet did the trick:

```
alter table customer delete statistics;
exec dbms_stats (…);
```

When the system immediately returned to an acceptable performance level, the DBA realized the importance of providing complete and timely statistics for the CBO using the *dbms_stats* utility.

Change CBO SQL Optimizer Parameters

In an emergency situation that involved an Oracle 9i client who was experiencing steadily degrading performance, their system was performing a large number of large-table, full-table scans which were suspected to be unnecessary. This suspicious information was found by a quick look into *v$sql_plan* view using the *plan9i.sql* script.

The top SQL was extracted from *v$sql* and timed as-is and with an index hint. While it was unclear why the CBO was not choosing the index, the query with the index hint ran almost 20x faster. After acting fast and running a script against *v$bh* and *user_indexes*, the DBA discovered that approximately 65 percent of the indexes were currently inside the data buffer cache.

Based on similar systems, the next step was to lower *optimizer_index_cost_adj* to a value of 20 in hopes of forcing the CBO to lower the relative costs of index access.

```
optimizer_index_cost_adj=20
optimizer_index_caching=65
```

Some parameters can be dynamically altered in versions of Oracle9i and newer.

```
alter system set optimizer_index_cost_adj=20 scope = pfile;
```

The execution plans for over 350 SQL statements were changed and the overall system response time was cut in half.

Repair Obsolete CBO Statistics Gathering

A client called and expressed confusion as to why their system was grinding to a halt. There was a serious degradation in SQL performance after the implementation of partitioned tablespaces in a 16-CPU Solaris 64-bit Oracle 9i system. The changes in the development and QA instances had been thoroughly tested.

As it turned out, analyze table and analyze index commands had been used to gather the CBO statistics. The *dbms_stats* utility gathers partition-wise statistics. There was not time to pull a deep sample collection, so a *dbms_stats* was issued with a 10 percent sample size. Note that it is parallelized with 15 parallel processes to speed up the statistics collection:

```
exec dbms_stats.gather_schema_stats ( -
   ownname           => 'SAPR4', -
   options           => 'GATHER AUTO', -
   estimate_percent  => 10, -
   method_opt        => 'for all columns size repeat', -
   degree            => 15 -
)
```

In less than 30 minutes, the improved CBO statistics tripled the performance of the entire database.

Conclusion

Oracle SQL tuning is the single most powerful silver bullet for the Oracle DBA, but it is also one of the most complex areas of Oracle tuning. The main points of this chapter include:

- Oracle tuning can be hindered by vendor packages, ad-hoc queries and dynamic SQL generation.

- Oracle has a wealth of SQL tuning tools for the DBA including optimizer plan stability, SQL profiles, optimizer parameters and CBO statistics.

- Oracle10g automates CBO statistics collection, but the cost-based optimizer has become even more complex with the new dynamic sampling and automatic histogram detection features.

- The top SQL tuning silver bullets include adjusting the CBO statistics, adding indexes and changing the optimizer parameters.

This book will conclude with a detailed look at Oracle hardware silver bullets.

Oracle Hardware
Silver Bullets

"We need faster hardware!"

Inside the Oracle Server

Once the DBA has optimized the Oracle instance, the only further hope for improvement in performance is applying faster hardware resources.

The rapid evolution of computing power has led to a narrowing of power between the traditional minicomputers and microcomputers. Just as the 16-bit architectures were replaced by 32-bit systems, today there are both proprietary UNIX and Windows operating systems offering robust 64-bit environments. For Oracle, this evolution gives the IT manager the freedom to

---

choose the architecture and operating system that best suits their business needs.

To fully understand the benefits of 64-bit processing, it is important to understand how the constant changes in CPU, RAM, and disk technology have affected database management over the past three decades. Once 64-bit processing is seen in its proper perspective, the benefits and shortcomings of using 64-bit Oracle servers become clear.

While an excessive amount of resource consumption may be due to a poorly optimized Oracle database, the perceptive Oracle tuning professional knows that the addition of hardware to a poorly tuned database is a legitimate economic tuning solution.

For example, tuning 5,000 SQL statements might cost $100,000 in human resources, but moving to faster 64-bit processors might only cost $20,000. Another example is a system that is heavily I/O-bound due to a poorly written application. Rebuilding the application might cost millions and take months, yet a move to super-fast solid-state disk can happen overnight at less cost. The application is still poorly written, but it runs many times faster.

It may not be elegant to throw hardware at an Oracle performance problem, but it can often be a cost-effective and timely solution to an acute Oracle tuning issue.

Once a database is fully tuned, faster CPU and solid-state disk (RAM-SAN) can further improve the throughput of the Oracle database.

There is a great debate about the rapidly-falling costs of hardware and the use of hardware resources as an Oracle tuning option.

The following sections will present some common skeptical comments.

Skeptic Comments

There is nothing wrong with disk I/O and full caching can hurt Oracle performance.

All Oracle10g world record benchmarks use over 50 Gigabyte data caches? Also, using multiple blocksizes has also helped greatly and the appropriate blocksize was used depending on the types of objects in the tablespaces.

For example, small OLTP access rows like a 2k blocksize because RAM isn't wasted hauling-in block space that is not needed. A 32k tablespace for index range scans also showed a large, measurable performance improvement:

The bigger your cache, the larger your LRU and Dirty List becomes.

This is true, but disk I/O is even more expensive! For example, check out the Sun Oracle 10g benchmark and their use of a 60 Gigabyte data buffer. The size of the buffer cache depends on the size of the working set of frequently referenced data! A very large OLTP system might need a 60 Gigabyte KEEP pool:

Also, the mechanism inside 10g AMM can be useful. It computes the marginal benefits of additional data block buffers based of the costs of less PIO and does indeed consider the costs of serialization overhead.

There comes a point where, for a particular unit of hardware, the marginal cost of the increase in administrative overhead

is greater than the marginal decrease in costs due to less physical I/O.

For reads, disk I/O is almost always shower then an LIO and full caching is great for read-only databases such as DSS, OLAP and DW systems! For write intensive databases, a large cache can be a problem. That's why many DBA's place high DML objects in a separate tablespace with a different blocksize, and map them to a smaller buffer.

Throwing more memory at the problem does NOT make it go away.

This statement can be generally true; however, hardware can make a sub-optimal database run far faster. For example, a client had a database and that was heavily I/O bound with 85% read waits. Instead of paying $100k in programmer costs to fix the root cause of the problem, they replaced the disks with high-speed RAM-SAN (solid-state disk) for only $40k. The system ran 15x faster, in less than 24 hours. Like it or not, disk will soon be as obsolete as drums devices.

While server overload conditions may indicate a sub-optimal Oracle component, it might just be that more hardware resources are needed.

For the moment, assume that there is an atrocious database loaded with sub-optimal SQL and inferior code. Is it legitimate to throw hardware at a bad code issue? The answer has to do more with economics than theory. For example, the database has thousands of sub-optimal SQL statements and 100,000 lines of poor PL/SQL. The database is heavily I/O bound with a large amount of unnecessary logical and physical I/O. Users might be presented with the following options:

- The code could be repaired for $50k in consulting and it would take 8 weeks; or.

- The tablespaces could be moved to a high-speed solid-state disk for $20k and be finished tomorrow.

If a hardware fix is used to address a software issue, the code will still be inefficient, but it might run 20x faster. The end result is still a cheaper solution. This approach is more common than one might think, and PC users might wonder why PC software consumes gobs of RAM and CPU.

The following section presents information on some of the external issues associated with Oracle performance.

Inside Oracle Server Bottlenecks

Many Oracle servers experience external bottlenecks for a variety of reasons. If SQL has not been completely optimized, the application makes excessive network calls, or the library cache has been configured improperly, a server overload condition could be experienced.

The following server overload conditions are most common for Oracle.

I/O Overload

This is evidenced by high "db file sequential read" and "db file scattered read" waits and can be detected in the Oracle10g *dba_hist_filestatxs* view. SQL that issues unnecessary table block access, possibly due to missing indexes or poor Cost Based Optimizer (CBO) statistics, should be investigated.

Assuming that the SQL is optimized, the only remaining solutions are the addition of RAM for the data buffers or the switch to solid-state disk.

CPU Overload

With the advent of 64-bit Oracle and super-large data block buffers such as *db_cache_size* and *db_keep_cache_size*, the main bottleneck for many databases has shifted from I/O to CPU. If the CPU is listed in the top wait events, SQL that may be causing unnecessary logical I/O against the data buffers should be investigated. The library cache can be investigated to see if excessive parsing might be causing the CPU consumption. Assuming that Oracle has been optimized, the options are to add more CPUs or faster CPU processors.

Network Overload

In many Oracle-based applications, the largest component of end-user response time is network latency. Oracle captures important metrics that will show if the Oracle database is network bound, specifically using the SQL*Net statistics from the *dba_hist_sysstat* view.

Because of the Oracle Transparent Network Substrate (TNS), there are only a few network tuning options (*sqlnet.ora*, *tnsnames.ora* and *listener.ora* parameters), and the network issues are usually external to the Oracle database.

RAM Overload

The Oracle10g Automatic Memory Management (AMM) utility has facilities such as *db_cache_size*, *shared_pool_size*, and *pga_aggregate_target,* in Oracle10g Enterprise Manager for detecting SGA regions that are too small.

RAM can be reallocated within these regions which will:

- reduce *pga_aggregate_target* if there are no disk sorts or hash joins

- reduce *shared_pool_size* if there is no library cache contention

- reduce *db_cache_size* if there is low disk I/O.

Historically, disk I/O was the premier wait event, but this has changed with the introduction of Solid State RAM disk and 64-bit Oracle where very large RAM data buffer caches can be implemented.

Disk I/O and Oracle

Oracle tuning techniques are modified to match changes to hardware technology. Having current tuning tools is especially important with a data storage application like Oracle. The cost and speed of disk devices have had a considerable impact on Oracle tuning.

In 1985, a 1.2 Gigabyte disk sold for more than $250,000. Today, users can buy 100 Gigabytes disks for $200 and 100 Gigabytes of RAM-disk for $100k. The following statements reflect truths about disk options:

- Disk storage improves 10x every year.

- Storage media becomes obsolete every 25 years.

- RAM-SAN will replace disks by 2006.

In Oracle, physical disk I/O can be measured from inside by querying STATSPACK and the AWR. The physical disk reads

---

information that is captured using the stats$filestatxs and dba dba_hist_filestatxs tables.

For example, the following Oracle 10g script detects all files with physical reads over 10,000 during the snapshot period:

🖫 high_phys_reads_10g.sql

```
-- ****************************************************
-- Copyright © 2005 by Rampant TechPress
-- This script is free for non-commercial purposes
-- with no warranties.  Use at your own risk.
--
-- To license this script for a commercial purpose,
-- contact info@rampant.cc
-- ****************************************************

break on begin_interval_time skip 2
column phyrds format 999,999,999
column begin_interval_time format a25

select
   begin_interval_time,
   filename,
   phyrds
from
   dba_hist_filestatxs
natural join
   dba_hist_snapshot
where
   phyrds > 10000
;
```

The results yield a running total of Oracle physical reads from phys_reads.sql. The snapshots are collected every hour in this example, and many DBAs will increase the default collection frequency of AWR snapshots. Starting from this script, users could easily add a where clause criteria and create a unique time-series exception report.

```
SQL> @phys_reads

BEGIN_INTERVAL_TIME FILENAME PHYRDS
----------------------- --------------------------------------- ------------
24-FEB-04 11.00.32.000 PM E:\ORACLE\ORA92\FSDEV10G\SYSTEM01.DBF     164,700
                          E:\ORACLE\ORA92\FSDEV10G\UNDOTBS01.DBF      26,082
                          E:\ORACLE\ORA92\FSDEV10G\SYSAUX01.DBF      472,008
                          E:\ORACLE\ORA92\FSDEV10G\USERS01.DBF        21,794
                          E:\ORACLE\ORA92\FSDEV10G\T_FS_LSQ.ORA       12,123

24-FEB-04 12.00.32.000 PM E:\ORACLE\ORA92\FSDEV10G\SYSTEM01.DBF     164,700
                          E:\ORACLE\ORA92\FSDEV10G\UNDOTBS01.DBF      26,082
```

This concept is particularly true if one recalls Moore's Law, which essentially states that device capacity increases steadily while hardware costs are falling.

The important exceptions to Moore's law are RAM chip characteristics. RAM is steadily falling in cost, but the speed has remained the same for more than 30 years, hovering at about 50 nanoseconds.

A Historical Perspective on Server Hardware

Back in the mid 1960's, Gordon Moore, the director of the research and development labs at Fairchild Semiconductor, published a research paper titled, *Cramming More Components into Integrated Circuits*. In his paper, Moore performed a linear regression on the rate of change in server processing speed and costs and noted an exponential growth in processing power and an exponential reduction of processing costs.

This landmark paper gave birth to "Moore's Law", which postulated that CPU power will get four times faster every three years. This phenomenon is illustrated in Figure 11.1.

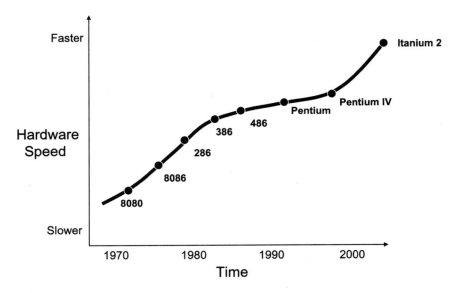

Figure 11.1: *Moore's Law for CPU speed.*

In the 1970's, a four-way Symmetric Multiprocessing (SMP) processor cost over three million dollars. Today, the same CPU can be purchased for under $3,000. CPUs will increase in speed four times every three years and only increase in cost by 50%.

While Moore's Law is generally correct, note that the curve is not linear. The formerly marginal rate of advances in CPU speed has increased dramatically in the past decade, most notably with the introduction of the Itanium2 processors.

The large RAM data buffers enabled by 64-bit operating systems have shifted the bottleneck for many Oracle databases from I/O to CPU. Oracle10g accommodates this shift to CPU consumption by providing a new *cpu_cost* feature that allows Oracle's cost-based SQL optimizer to evaluate SQL execution plan costs based on predicted CPU costs rather than I/O costs. This is an optional feature in Oracle10g and must be manually enabled.

Even though it is true that a CPU bottleneck exists when the run queue exceeds the number of processors, this condition does not always mean that the best solution is to add processors. Excessive CPU load can be caused by many internal conditions including inefficient SQL statements that perform excessive logical I/O, non-reentrant SQL inside the library cache, and many other conditions.

Fortunately, Oracle 10g Enterprise Manager allows users to look back in time and find these conditions, even though the immediate run queue issue has passed.

While Moore's law is quite correct for processor speed and cost, many have over generalized this principle as it applies to disks and RAM. It is true that costs are continually falling for RAM and disk, but the speed assumptions do not necessarily apply, as illustrated in Figure 11.2.

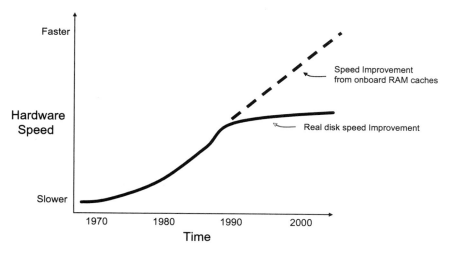

Figure 11.2: *Moore's Law for Disk speed.*

This is a very different curve. The old-fashioned spinning platters of magnetic-coated metal have an upper limit of spin speed, and the read-write head movement speed is limited. In the early 1990's, it became apparent that the 1950's disk technology had peaked. It became necessary for disk manufacturers to add on-board RAM caches to disk arrays and include asynchronous writing mechanisms to continue to improve disk speed.

One glaring exception to Moore's law is RAM speed as shown in Figure 11.3.

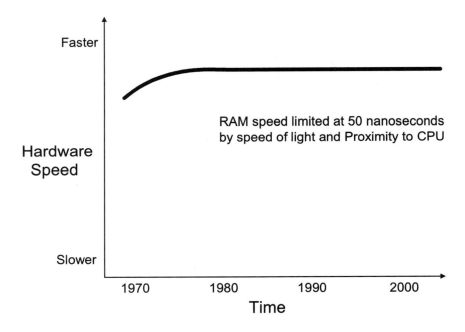

Figure 11.3: *Moore's Law for RAM speed.*

RAM has not made any measurable gain in speed since the mid 1970's. This is due to the limitations of silicon and the fact that access speed in nanoseconds approaches the speed of light. The only way to further improve the speed of RAM would be to employ a radical new medium such as Gallium Arsenide.

This flat speed curve for RAM has important ramifications to Oracle processing. Since CPU speed continues to outpace RAM speed, RAM sub-systems must be localized to keep the CPUs running at full capacity. This type of approach is evident in the new Itanium2 servers where the RAM is placed as close to the CPU as possible as shown in Figure 11.4.

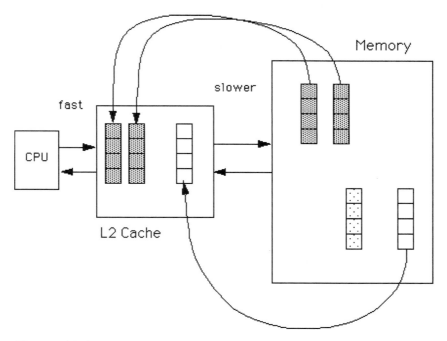

Figure 11.4: *Localizing RAM in 64-bit Servers.*

This represents the Oracle servers of the 21st century (e.g. the UNISYS ES7000, the Sun Superdome) which have a special "L2" RAM that is placed near the processors for super-fast RAM access.

In sum, RAM technology has dramatically changed the way that Oracle databases are tuned.

Server RAM and Oracle

Today, 100 Gigabytes of RAM-Disk can be purchased for as little as $100,000 and can deliver access times 6,000 times faster than traditional disk devices. By 2013, a Gigabyte of RAM is projected to cost the same as a Gigabyte of disk today, which is approximately $200.

RAM I/O bandwidth is projected to grow one bit every 18 months, making a 128 bit architecture due in about 2010 as shown in Table 11.1.

8 bit	1970's
16 bit	1980's
32 bit	1990's
64 bit	2000's
128 bit	2010's

Table 11.1: *RAM bandwidth evolution.*

The fact that RAM does not get faster means that CPU speed continues to outpace memory speed. This means that RAM subsystems must be localized to keep the CPUs running at full capacity. Fortunately, the AWR can be used to track these important external server metrics.

Tracking External Server Metrics with AWR

Oracle sets several important initialization parameters based on the numbers of CPUs on the Oracle sever and is now more mindful of the costs of CPU cycles and I/O operations. Indeed, with each new release of Oracle, the database becomes more in tune to its external environment.

Further, 64-bit Oracle servers have changed Oracle server metric tuning activities for the DBA.

Oracle and the 64-Bit Server Technology

The advent of 64-bit CPUs has led to a great change in the way that Oracle databases are managed and tuned. To understand the issues, one must understand the advantages of a 64-bit server, especially the ability to have super-large data buffer caches. The following are the architectural benefits of the 64-bit processors listed in order of importance to Oracle shops:

- **Improved RAM Addressing** - Sadly a 32-bit word size can only address approximately 4 Gigabytes of RAM (2 to the 32nd power). All 64-bit servers have a larger word size that allows for up to 18 billion Gigabytes (2 to the 64th power or 18 exabytes). These servers allow for huge scalability as the processing demand grows.

- **Faster Processors** - Intel's 64-bit Itanium2 architecture is more powerful than the older 32-bit chipsets. While faster chips are not a direct result of the 64-bit architecture, they are an important consideration for shops with computationally intensive databases.

- **High Parallelism** - Multiple CPU and SMP support allows large scale parallel processing. For example, the Unisys 64-bit ES7000 servers support up to 32 processors which yields large parallel benefits.

- **Cluster Architecture** - The 64-bit servers, such as the Unisys 64-bit ES7000 servers, are generally cluster ready.

While having a 64-bit processor might be an attractive option, a large number of Oracle shops continued to run 32-bit versions of the Oracle database on their servers. The new Intel processor architectures now rivals the proprietary UNIX systems with the ability to house CPUs and over 20 Gigabytes of RAM capacity. This architecture is shown in Figure 11.5. This architecture can support thousands of users while providing sub-second response time.

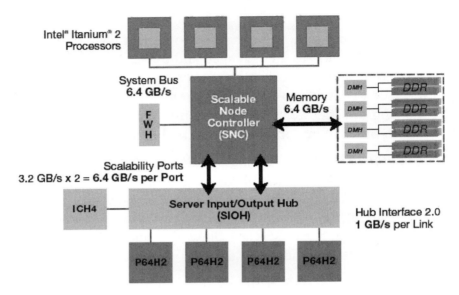

Figure 11.5: *The Intel E8870 Chipset supporting the Itanium 2 processor.*

Intel also allows architecture to be scaled to a 16-way SMP configuration as shown in Figure 11.6. It becomes apparent that Intel will continue to pursue the hardware level expansion of this architecture.

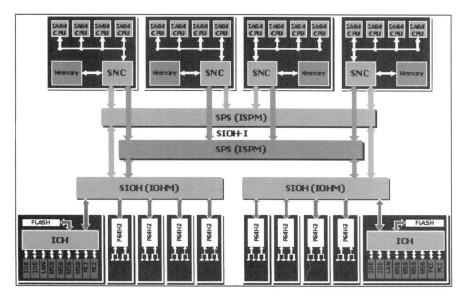

Figure 11.6: *The 16-way Itanium 2 architecture (Courtesy UNISYS).*

With the 32-way and 64-way megaservers, there is now a server architecture reminiscent of the larger servers offered by Sun, HP and IBM. As all the vendors are offering 64-bit servers, the greatest benefit to Oracle shops occurs in these areas:

- **High Transactions Processing Rates** - For systems with more than 200 disk I/Os per second, disk I/O is reduced by caching large amounts of data and system performance skyrockets.

- **Declining Performance** - The 32-bit limitations prevent continued growth beyond a certain point. The 64-bit architecture raises the ceiling on that growth.

- **Anticipating Rapid Growth** - For systems that require uninterrupted growth and scalability, the 64-bit architecture allows almost infinite scalability. Many large Enterprise Resource Planning (ERP) systems have been able to scale successfully on Windows 64 platforms.

- **Computationally-Intensive System** - If an Oracle database is CPU-bound or if it performs multiple parallel full-table scans, the faster processors in a 64-bit architecture are very appealing.

So what does this mean to the Oracle professional? Larry Ellison, CEO of Oracle, noted at OracleWorld in 2003:

"If you want the world's faster processors then you will be forced to pay less."

He was referring to the Intel Itanium2 chips which appear to be making strong advances in the displacement of the proprietary UNIX environments, especially HP/UX and Solaris. The major operating environments for Itanium2 servers are Linux and Microsoft Windows:

- **Linux** - Offers large scale uptake but is hindered by non-open source costs (Red Hat) and lackluster support.

- **Windows** - Increasing in popularity but suffering from unreliable past performance.

These large inexpensive servers provide the ultimate in resource sharing. With many Oracle instances on a single server, processes that need more CPU will automatically be allocated cycles from the server run queue. Likewise, an instance that requires additional RAM for the SGA or PGA can easily get the resources without cumbersome manual intervention.

In summary, 16-way and 32-way SMP servers are leading the way into a new age of Oracle database consolidation.

Oracle Data Warehouse Hardware

All of these techniques have helped to remove I/O bottlenecks and to make data warehouse applications more CPU intensive. There are many server resources that are required for all large data warehouse applications. These features include:

- **Large RAM Regions** - All 64-bit servers have a larger word size (two to the 64th power) that allows for up to 18 billion GB (that's 18 exabytes). This allows for huge scalability as the processing demand grows and allows the database to have many Gigabytes of data buffer storage.

- **Fast CPU** - Intel's 64-bit Itanium2 architecture is far faster than the older 32-bit chipsets. The advanced features built into the Itanium2 chipset allow much more real work to be done for each processor cycle. When combined with the Oracle10g NUMA RAM, computationally intensive DSS queries run at lightening speeds.

- **High Parallelism** - Each processing node has four Itanium2 CPUs interconnected to local memory modules and an inter-node crossbar interconnect controller via a high-speed bus. Up to four of these processing nodes can be interconnected, creating a highly scalable SMP system. This design allows large scale parallel processing for Oracle full-table scans. These scattered reads are the hallmark of Oracle warehouse systems. For example, the new 64-bit servers support up to 64 processors, allowing for large parallel benefits.

- **High Performance I/O Architecture** - The I/O subsystem also influences scalability and performance. Enterprise systems must provide the channel capacity required to support large databases and networks. The Itanium2 system architecture can support up to 64 peripheral component interconnect (PCI or PCI-X) 64-bit channels operating at speeds from 33 MHz to 100 MHz.

The Scale-Up Approach

Most savvy Oracle shops practice the scale-up approach first, and then they scale-out. There is a common misconception that using a single server with scale-up capabilities introduces a single-point-of-failure problem. In reality, hardware redundancy on the new mega-servers offers full protection against failure:

- Redundant cooling, power, and dual air conditioning.

- On-board power management.

- Hot-pluggable components.

- Full parity checking.

- Distributed power.

- Automated failure diagnosis and recovery.

- Proactive failover.

The scale-up approach is the natural reaction to the rampant distribution of Oracle systems onto small, independent servers. This architecture saves money on hardware costs, but at the expense of hiring a huge system administration and DBA staff. This is the appeal of consolidation: to avoid the high overhead and expense of such server farms.

Because of the advances in server technology, the concept of using a large server has become very popular. Here is an approach used by many forward-thinking Oracle shops:

- First we scale-up within a single SMP server:

- On-demand resource allocation by sharing CPU and RAM between many resources.

- Less maintenance and human resources to manage fewer servers.

- Optimal utilization of RAM and CPU resources.

- High availability through fault-tolerant components.

- Next we scale-out with multiple SMP servers using RAC:

- High availability through clustering servers with RAC.

- Optimal utilization of servers.

- Quicker implementation and easier maintenance with fewer servers.

This approach provides a high degree of scalability and flexibility for high performance and also provides high availability and low cost of ownership (TCO).

Again, the scale-out approach is designed for super-large Oracle databases that support many thousands of concurrent users. Unless there is a need to support more than 10,000 transactions per second then it is likely that it would be better to use a scale-up approach.

Amazon is an excellent example of a scale-out Oracle shop. Amazon announced that their intention is to move their 14 trillion byte Oracle database to Oracle RAC on Linux. Amazon uses load-balanced Linux Web servers to horizontally scale its Web presence. The savings from the switch to Linux has also allowed Amazon to enhance the fault tolerance of its infrastructure.

Add Faster CPU

When a client with a computationally intensive scientific application was complaining of constantly degrading response time, a review of the data buffers using *v$db_cache_advice*

---

confirmed that the working set of frequently referenced data was buffered, yet CPU consumption was at the top wait event in the report:

```
Top 5 Timed Events
                                                       % Total
Event                           Waits    Time (s) Ela Time
------------------------------- -------- -------- --------
CPU time                           4,851    4,042    55.76
db file sequential read            1,968    1,997    27.55
log file sync                    299,097      369     5.08
db file scattered read            53,031      330     4.55
log file parallel write          302,680      190     2.62
```

A review of the server *vmstat* data confirmed that the run queue for the application exceeded the number of processors on the server. In this case, the run queue column of *vmstat* was always greater than eight, the number of processors on the server:

```
root> vmstat 2 5

kthr     memory            page                   faults           cpu
----- ---------- ------------------------ ------------ -----------
 r  b     avm   fre  re  pi  po  fr   sr cy   in    sy   cs  us sy id wa
 7  5  220214   141   0   0   0  42   53  0 1724 12381 2206  19 46 28  7
 9  5  220933   195   0   0   1 216  290  0 1952 46118 2712  27 55 13  5
13  5  220646   452   0   0   1  33   54  0 2130 86185 3014  30 59  8  3
 9  5  220228   672   0   0   0   0    0  0 1929 25068 2485  25 49 16 10
```

In this case, the database was migrated to a new 64-bit server with Linux, running the super-fast Itanium2 chipset. After the migration the end users reported that a four hour analytical process was running in less than 20 minutes and the overall application ran more than four times faster.

Add Solid-State Disk

There was a data warehouse that client who complained that increasing data load volumes were causing their batch load windows to grow to eight hours. A review of the top-5 wait events confirmed that the database was heavily disk I/O bound:

```
Top 5 Timed Events
                                                      % Total
Event                          Waits    Time (s) Ela Time
------------------------   ------------ ----------- --------
db file sequential read         2,598     7,146     48.54
db file scattered read         25,519     3,246     22.04
library cache load lock           673     1,363      9.26
CPU time                           44     1,154      7.83
log file parallel write        19,157       837      5.68
```

As a test, solid-state disks were used in the data loading partition. The rows per second insert rate is shown below in Figure 11.7, and the data load rate increased by 66%, taking the four hour loads window down to less than 90 minutes.

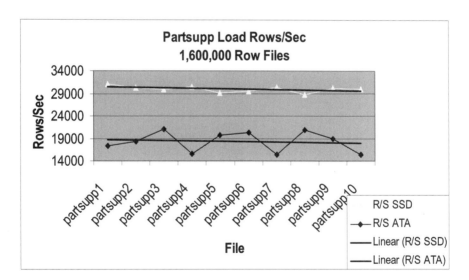

Figure 11.7: *Example Rows per Second Comparison.*

In this case, the SSD drives loaded 66 percent more rows per second. SSD technology is also wonderful for write-intensive data files such as the Oracle redo log and TEMP tablespace.

Conclusion

This chapter has dealt with Oracle hardware silver bullets and demonstrated how the intelligent use of hardware resources can speed-up Oracle system performance. The main points of this chapter include:

- Hardware is the only Oracle tuning option after the instance, application code and SQL have been optimized.

- Some managers are choosing to apply hardware resources to suboptimal Oracle systems because of the reduced risk and lower costs.

- Solid-state RAM Disk is rapidly displacing traditional disks and is now used to relieve I/O contention with Oracle databases.

- Faster CPU's have greatly aided computationally intensive Oracle applications.

Book Conclusion

This book has introduced a holistic approach to Oracle tuning and focused on a top-down approach to tuning, using broad-brush techniques to optimize as much of the database as possible. The main points of this book include:

- **Oracle Tuning is Dynamic** - All Oracle databases are constantly changing and there is no once-and-for-all tuning solution. All Oracle tuning must be proactive and time-based.

- **Use a Top-Down Tuning Strategy** - Savvy Oracle tuning professionals start with broad-brush techniques to tune as much of the whole database as possible before starting time-consuming and expensive application and SQL tuning.

- **Know the Silver Bullets** - Single changes like adding an index or changing an Oracle parameter can have a dramatic impact on the performance of your database.

This book has not been intended as a substitute for a proper application and SQL tuning. Instead, it addresses the common reality that the Oracle DBA may not have the luxury of addressing the root causes of performance issues such as vendor SQL, a bad database design or a sub-optimal application.

As always, reader comments and suggestions are welcome so that this, and future books, can be improved. Please feel free to contact me at info@rampant.cc.

Regards,

Donald K. Burleson

Index

About Don Burleson

Don Burleson is one of the world's top Oracle Database experts with more than 20 years of full-time DBA experience. He specializes in creating database architectures for very large online databases and he has worked with some of the world's most powerful and complex systems.

A former Adjunct Professor, Don Burleson has written 32 books, published more than 100 articles in National Magazines, and serves as Editor-in-Chief of Oracle Internals and Senior Consulting Editor for DBAZine and Series Editor for Rampant TechPress. Don is a popular lecturer and teacher and is a frequent speaker at OracleWorld and other international database conferences.

As a leading corporate database consultant, Don has worked with numerous Fortune 500 corporations creating robust database architectures for mission-critical systems. Don is also a noted expert on eCommerce systems, and has been instrumental in the development of numerous Web-based systems that support thousands of concurrent users.

In addition to his services as a consultant, Don also is active in charitable programs to aid visually impaired individuals. Don pioneered a technique for delivering tiny pigmy horses as guide animals for the blind and manages a non-profit corporation called the Guide Horse Foundation dedicated to providing Guide horses to blind people free-of-charge. The Web Site for The Guide Horse Foundation is www.guidehorse.org.

About Mike Reed

When he first started drawing, Mike Reed drew just to amuse himself. It wasn't long, though, before he knew he wanted to be an artist. Today he does illustrations for children's books, magazines, catalogs, and ads.

He also teaches illustration at the College of Visual Art in St. Paul, Minnesota. Mike Reed says, "Making pictures is like acting — you can paint yourself into the action." He often paints on the computer, but he also draws in pen and ink and paints in acrylics. He feels that learning to draw well is the key to being a successful artist.

Mike is regarded as one of the nation's premier illustrators and is the creator of the popular "Flame Warriors" illustrations at www.flamewarriors.com, a website devoted to Internet insults. "To enter his Flame Warriors site is sort of like entering a hellish Sesame Street populated by Oscar the Grouch and 83 of his relatives." – Los Angeles Times. (http://redwing.hutman.net/%7Emreed/warriorshtm/lat.htm)

Mike Reed has always enjoyed reading. As a young child, he liked the Dr. Seuss books. Later, he started reading biographies and war stories. One reason why he feels lucky to be an illustrator is because he can listen to books on tape while he works. Mike is available to provide custom illustrations for all manner of publications at reasonable prices. Mike can be reached at www.mikereedillustration.com.

Free!
Oracle 10g Senior DBA Reference Poster

This 24 x 36 inch quick reference includes the important data columns and relationships between the DBA views, allowing you to quickly write complex data dictionary queries.

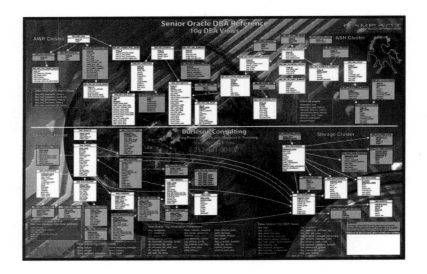

This comprehensive data dictionary reference contains the most important columns from the most important Oracle10g DBA views. Especially useful are the Automated Workload Repository (AWR) and Active Session History (ASH) DBA views.

WARNING - This poster is not suitable for beginners. It is designed for senior Oracle DBAs and requires knowledge of Oracle data dictionary internal structures. You can get your poster at this URL:

www.rampant.cc/poster.htm